Eddie Smotherman

BODY POLITICS

Five Practices of the Christian Community Before the Watching World

John Howard Yoder

DISCIPLESHIP RESOURCES
MATERIALS FOR GROWTH IN CHRISTIAN FAITH AND LIFE

P.O. Box 189 • Nashville, TN 37202 • Phone (615) 340-7284

Library of Congress Card Catalog No. 92-71308

ISBN 0-88177-118-X

DR118

CONTENTS

PREFACE

I owe special gratitude to those in whose company these themes were first treated in something like this form:

—To Professor Geoffrey Wainwright, thanks to whose invitation the original lecture, from whom this entire outline was developed, was presented at Duke University Divinity School;

—To David McConnell of the United Methodist Yellowstone Conference and to Larry Harvey of Central Kansas for the privilege of participating in their respective district Pastors' Schools and for their encouragement to make further use of the material;

—To Ingrid Christiansen and Jody Kretzmann of Holden Village for the opportunity to review these same materials while renewing our family's bond with the Village's unique brand of Lutheranism.

I thank Editor Craig Gallaway of Discipleship Resources for deciding that this kind of treatment of some generally neglected themes could find a place in Discipleship Resources.

In other ways I owe gratitude to United Methodist pastors Sara and Ed Phillips and Laurel and Augustus Jordan for making United Methodism tangible to me in "Michiana" and for commending this material to the editors of Discipleship Resources. The Reverends Jordan have helped me as well to make the text a little more readable.

Stanley Hauerwas and Michael Cartwright were helpful when they warned me that a semi-popular treatment of these themes should (and could) avoid raising as a barrier the academically "prior" questions of theological method.

A briefer and more technical presentation of these same themes, after being read as a single lecture in seminaries, was published in the April 1991 issue of *Theology Today*. I have also treated some of the themes elsewhere, some at greater length, some with a different emphasis. I shall provide references to some of those other texts, but have not sought to be exhaustive.

John H. Yoder
Notre Dame, Indiana
Pentecost 1992

INTRODUCTION

Before moving to the substance of our study, the reader might be helped by a brief explanation of the frame of reference of the entire series, with the intentionally ambivalent term *Politics* in its title.

There seems to be no end of debating about how the church should be or should not be "involved" in "politics." An example: In 1989 when South Africa's most important black leader, Nelson Mandela, just out of prison, visited the Pope to ask him to support the idea of economic sanctions against the apartheid regime of his native South Africa, John Paul II said he could not do that because it would be "political." So "political" meant somehow, in that one case, something with which the head of the Roman Catholic Church should not be involved. Yet such concerns had never kept him from multiple interventions in the public life of his own native Poland when he was an archbishop there.

Different denominational traditions and different fractional groups within denominations talk past one another with intense conviction about what is "political" and what is not, usually without examining how the terms they use with such confidence are defined. Some think that "involvement in politics" should (and therefore can) be avoided by the church, at least by pastors, if not by Christian citizens. *Politics* means what governments do or what "politicians" do, and "church" people can avoid that. Others argue that such avoidance is not possible or would not be right, because Christians should be concerned with all of life, "politics" not excluded. Most elected politicians in the United States and Canada are church members who believe that being involved in political matters is a good thing for Christians to do, but then there is a new debate about how their two memberships are related. John F. Kennedy notoriously proclaimed, when a candidate for the United States presidency, that his being a Roman Catholic would make no difference in how he would discharge his office.

Thus the recently dominant understanding of things has assumed that there is a vast qualitative distance between the realm we call "politics" and the one we call "church." The Mandela/pope anecdote illustrates this understanding and its limits. The notion of separation is often especially thought to apply to that part of the "church" realm usually called "worship," which usually means whatever it is that the church does that is the most important. Like the other common words we have been using, *worship* usually means certain special set-apart activities that belong in their own realm. Ask yourself whether this is not in fact what you have thought. Is "worship" not something that by nature belongs in another realm than that of ordinary life?

There are ways to bridge that chasm between "church" and "politics" or between "worship" and ordinary life, many people will say, but all agree that a bridge is needed. Then they differ about what the right bridge is. From the perspective called "liberal," the bridge between the two is thought to be a set of *insights* concerning human nature and the world, such ideas as justice and freedom and understandings of why and how we should behave. Worship is then thought of as inculcating such insights and reinforcing devotion to them. Worship helps you understand things in a particular way; then, in the light of those understandings, you will be usefully active in public affairs. It will, for instance, help you think of the global ecology as something God created for a purpose or of your neighbor's hunger as your responsibility. Those understandings will guide you to act.

For the perspective sometimes called "pietist," the bridge is held to be a new set of *"insides"*—the Hebrews said "bowels," the Latins "heart." These figures of speech are used to designate something deep within which makes a person what he or she is, something like "will" or "motivation." Here the concept is that worship modifies the composition of the person on such levels as guilt, self-esteem, and love in such a way that the changed person will behave differently and thereby change the world. If you are less bothered by feelings of guilt, you may be more able to take risks. If you are more consciously filled by a sense of the love of God, you may care more about the needy and be more motivated to serve them. If you are more disposed to trust God for your welfare, you may be freed to be more generous.

The realm called "politics" or "the real world" is thought of, according to both accounts, as being in some ultimate sense secondary to the word and work of God with which worship deals. The "nonpolitical" realm is in some "spiritual" sense "prior."

At the same time, however, the values with which "politics" deals are considered to be "autonomous." Political moral insight is a law unto itself, independent. Such values are nature, reason, law. They are considered autonomous in that they are thought to be known otherwise than through revelation or worship.[1] Nature, reason, and law are all concepts we assume we share with all our neighbors. Ordinarily the definitions of such concepts do not seem to be dependent on faith or on Jesus, although maybe we hold them to be vaguely supported by nature or "nature's God." In any case, we do not expect "worship" to tell us more about them.

These values are also thought to be autonomous, able to stand alone as to substance and to what they call us to do. The duties they lay upon us are different from what Jesus calls us to do. For example, a banker is called to save money or to lend it with interest, not to give it away or to lend it without interest. A soldier in battle is not supposed to love the enemy.

One of the most widely represented ways of describing this "autonomy" of the rules we should follow in the political realm is the "doctrine of creation." According to this doctrine, some say that we can know what God's will is by looking at the shape of the world as it is. We look at the family, the school, the factory, the marketplace, the state, and so on. Each of these structures defines the obligations of individuals in their respective slots.[2] Then the "calling" or "vocation" of the individual is to fit into that "station" or "role" and to act accordingly.

Now we could study that notion of autonomy somewhat abstractly, as a question in the realm of systematic theology. But in this study we are rather going to test that notion by bypassing it and returning to a larger question. Instead of turning to general concepts such as creation and vocation, we shall be asking, on the basis of the New Testament texts, about particular kinds of behavior that our faith requires.

The theme of separation and autonomy is not the question this study is pursuing. I have begun by describing it, in a prefatory way, because the reader will recognize that it is the way things are often described. If I were called upon, in some other setting, to discuss that question for its own sake, I would need to argue on theological grounds that it is inadequately posed. If you ask the wrong question, you may not be able to get the right answer.

Here, however, I set aside any effort to analyze that debate by further picking away at the various definitions of terms such as *involve* or *political* and *creation* or *reason*.

Instead, this study will pick up the topic of the church as body, for its own sake, from the beginning. The Christian community, like any community held together by commitment to important values, *is* a political reality. That is, the church has the character of a *polis* (the Greek word from which we get the adjective *political*), namely, a structured social body. It has its ways of making decisions, defining membership, and carrying out common tasks. That makes the Christian community a political entity in the simplest meaning of the term.

This study will show, pursuing several independent but convergent lines, that there is another way to relate what is usually called two "realms." We shall see this other pattern falling into place, inductively, as the exploration proceeds.

Stated very formally, the pattern we shall discover is that the will of God for human socialness as a whole is prefigured by the shape to which the Body of Christ is called. Church and world are not two compartments under separate legislation or two institutions with contradictory assignments, but two levels of the pertinence of the same Lordship. The people of God is called to be today what the world is called to be ultimately.

First, then, we shall review, in an intentionally simple way,[3] how the Christian community itself[4] is a political entity. The church's calling to be faithful in God's service is definable in political terms. It will then become evident that the issue of involvement in the structural processes of the wider society (education, economy, civil order, and so on) does not have the simple bipolar shape, creating the problem of how to get from one to the other, which the argument we noted at the outset always assumed.

The first meaning of the title *Body Politics* is thus that it obligates us to deal with the life of the church in ordinary human language, asking how that set of relationships which Paul called Christ's body is to function as a social organism, a *polis*.[5] To be political is to make decisions, to assign roles, and to distribute powers, and the Christian community cannot do otherwise than exercise these same functions, going about its business as a body.

The phrase found in the title, *body politics*, is of course partly redundant. It is not that there could be *bodiless politics* or *apolitical bodies*. Yet each term does say more than the other would alone. "Politics" affirms an unblinking recognition that we deal with matters of power, of rank and of money, of costly decisions and dirty hands, of memories and feelings. The difference between church and state or between a faithful and an unfaithful church is not that one is political and the other not, but that they are political in different ways.

"Body" is an ancient image for the human community. When I use it as a modifier, it pins down the awareness that each member needs and serves each of the others, that the whole is more than all of the parts, and that the interdependence of all is structured according to an already given plan, flexible and able to grow, but neither chaotic nor infinitely negotiable.

As the subtitle indicates, our study will focus on five sample ways in which the Christian church is called to operate as a *polis*. There could well be others, but the five cases should suffice to make the pattern clear. Our model in each case will be the practice of the early church as reflected in the writings of the New Testament.

The learnings we shall be reviewing about the practices of the early Christians will not be very novel or very complex. I shall also be concerned, however, to pay attention to the way the learnings all hang together, the way the themes, though quite independent, are formally parallel. Around each of our five topics we shall see that there is a social practice lived out by the early Christians, under divine mandate, which at the same time offers a paradigm for the life of the larger society. Each of the themes, moreover, calls into question in its own way the traditional understanding of the realm of sacrament, which has often stood in the way of believers' understanding of their faith as a phenomenon in and for "the real world."

Our agenda is ecumenical, not in the modern organizational sense of arranging conversations among denominational agencies, or in the sense of comparing and contrasting the foundational documents of conflicting confessions, but in the simpler sense of being relevant to all kinds of Christians. It is quite congenial with the original "methodism" of the Wesleys and with the cell movements fostered by Methodist campus ministries in the 1950s and the Covenant Discipleship movement being promoted in United Methodism today; yet there is nothing peculiarly Methodist about it. I shall occasionally provide illustrations not only from the New Testament but also from the Protestant Reformation of the sixteenth century. It has its Roman Catholic instances and counterparts as well and its nondenominational ones, but I shall make no effort to report on them all.

One last prefatory comment: The following studies reach back to the texts of the New Testament, as they stand. The words of Jesus, the narratives of Acts, and the instructions of the Apostles are taken straightforwardly here for what they seem to say in the text as it has come down to us. This should not be misunderstood as a "fundamentalist" disregard for the awareness, heightened by scholarship in recent generations, that all of these ancient texts probably underwent change in the process of oral transmission and rewriting through the early decades of the church. A fuller study would properly deal with the great diversity among the canonical texts themselves and the still greater diversity which must have characterized all of the early churches.[6] The fact that these texts make sense *for our purposes* as they stand does not imply any naive disregard for the questions scholars ask about how the traditions were passed on or how the texts as they now stand got written or what else other Christians at the same time were thinking and doing. Seldom however will variant scholarly perspectives on those matters throw any seriously different light on our understanding of the early Christian practices. I could say it more strongly: Only modern scholarship, with its more careful concern for reading ancient texts in their setting and liberating them from the assumption that what they are about is the same as what all Christians have already been thinking, has made possible the straightforwardness with which the readings at the core of the present study will proceed. Only the awareness of diversity and change has made it possible to ask where the trajectory of a given idea began and what the Good News at its core was then.

1

Binding and Loosing

The simplest way to designate the first practice of the early Christians, at which we shall be looking, is to use Jesus' own words, namely *binding* and *loosing*. But we need to unpack what he meant.

> If your brother or sister sins,[7]
> go and reprove that person
> when the two of you are alone.
> If he or she listens,
> you have won your brother or sister.
> (Matt. 18:15)[8]

In this key passage of Matthew's Gospel, Jesus instructed his disciples that when they would carry out this particular practice, following these simple instructions, their activity would at the same time be the activity of God. "What you bind on earth is bound in heaven," he said (Matt. 18:18).

Jesus thereby mandated a specific human activity, describing in some detail how it should proceed. God would at the same time be acting "in, with, and under"[9] that human activity. When human and divine activity coincide in this way, that is what some denominations call a *sacrament*. Baptists[10] and the Churches of Christ, concerned to avoid superstitious or mechanical misunderstandings, call it an *ordinance*. We have no reason to argue about the label, but we need to pursue further what the activity is that can have that significance.

The context in Matthew 18, reinforced by the parallel in John 20:23—"If you retain the sins of any, they are retained"—makes it clear that one objective or one outcome of this procedure is forgiveness, "remitting" an offense, reconciliation, "winning" the

1

brother or sister, restoring to the community a person who had
offended. That is part of what it means when you go to your sister
or brother and your conversation "wins" that person.[11]

Yet Jesus' choice of a pair of rabbinic technical terms, *bind* and
loose, indicates that more than that is involved. To "bind" in
rabbinic usage is to respond to a question of ethical discernment:
We still have the root in our word *obligate.* To "loose" is to free
from obligation: In the beginning of the Sermon on the Mount,
Jesus had warned that whoever "looses" any commandment will
be "the least in the kingdom." Thus the activity has two dimensions: moral discernment and reconciliation.

Into the interlocking of the dialogue of reconciliation with the
dialogue of moral discernment, Jesus inserted yet another element of classical due process. According to Mosaic law (Num.
35:30; Deut. 17:6; 19:15; John 8:17), it took "two witnesses" to
make a serious judicial deliberation valid. Jesus said that the
participants in this process of discernment and/or reconciliation
are doing that when they come together in his name and
"harmonize" (the verb is *symphonein,* which we recognize in the
noun form "symphony"). This congregational procedure is, in
other words, a counterpart of the way God authorized ancient
Israel to deal with moral and legal matters.

The same thought came up once before in Matthew's Gospel
where Jesus gave his disciples the authority to bind and loose
(16:19). These are the only places where he used the word *ecclesia,* which we translate "church." The original meaning of the
word *ecclesia* is political; it is literally a "called meeting," an
assembly, such as a town meeting, convened to do business, to
deliberate on behalf of the entire society.

Jesus described in surprising detail the conversational process
for which he was calling. Three efforts at reconciliation must be
made before accepting the fact that the offender refuses to be
"won." As a pastoral process, this differs significantly from some
understandings of community discipline:

   a. The initiative is personal, not a clergy function. The one who is to address the offender is the person who knows about the offense, not a clergyperson.

b. The intention is restorative, not punitive.

c. There is no distinction between major offenses and minor ones: Any offense is forgivable, but none is trivial.

d. The intention is not to protect the church's reputation or to teach onlookers the seriousness of sin, but only to serve the offender's own well-being by restoring her or him to the community.

Once the conclusion is reached, its validity is more than human: "What you bind on earth is bound in heaven." The community's action is God's action. This corrects for an anticatholic bias to which we in the free churches are prone; we have tended to deny that one human can forgive another in God's name. We have tended to assume or even to argue that anyone who has heard the Gospel words can appropriate them by an inward mental action— can forgive herself or himself. This point is correct halfway in that it denies that the authority to forgive is the *monopoly* of the priesthood. Yet there is no promise that offense can be reconciled without person-to-person process or that I can forgive myself. Reconciliation is between two parties; one of them cannot do it alone.

The parallel in John 20 makes the authority point even more strongly: "As the Father has sent me, so I send you" (v. 21). Jesus acted out the empowerment by breathing on them: "Receive the Holy Breath." That Jesus claimed to be sent by the Father had already offended contemporary leaders; now he "sends" the disciples. It was even more offensive that he forgave people. Yet even that function was passed on to the disciples: "If you forgive the sins of any, they are forgiven them; if you retain the sins of any, they are retained" (v. 23).

Some versions of the Matthew text read "if your brother or sister sins *against you*." Those two words, only five letters in the Greek, can be interpreted as limiting this reconciling process to cases of personal offense. This misdirects attention away from concern for the restoration of the offender and toward the feelings of the offended one. Those five letters are neither in the oldest manuscripts of Matthew nor in the parallel in Luke 17:3. If I am not the one sinned against, this fact may make it more difficult for me to recognize my responsibility to intervene, but it may also make it easier for me to be forgiving and evenhanded. The person offended is not excused from the responsibility to reconcile; yet neither is anyone else who knows about it.

"Forgive us our sins as we forgive others" is the only petition in the Lord's Prayer to be conditional and the only part of the prayer to which Jesus added comments (Matt. 6:14,15). The same linkage between our forgiving each other and God's forgiving us is restated elsewhere in the New Testament:

> ". . . forgiving one another, as God in Christ has forgiven you"
>
> (Eph. 4:32)

> ". . . just as the Lord has forgiven you, so you also must forgive"
>
> (Col. 3:13)

Paul referred to this process as "the law of Christ." He appealed to those of his readers who were "spiritual" to initiate it "in a spirit of gentleness," in the awareness of their own weakness (Gal. 6:1). As he urged the believers in Corinth not to litigate in pagan courts (1 Cor. 6:1-8), one of the reasons he gave was that there should be some wise mediator in their midst. That is an application of the same principle. The Epistle of James ends with another call to the same process (5:19,20).

In the light of experience, we know that this process needs to be defended against some serious abuses. We noted already that the intention is winning the brother or sister, not punishment. It is not defending the community's reputation or teaching a lesson to youth about the wrongness of sin. It is not confirming the authority of a congregation's leadership; in fact, it is not a ministerial prerogative at all. It is not, as some have thought, a procedure to be used on small sins, whereby big ones would be dealt with more strictly. It is not, as others have argued, to be used only on big public sins, while leaving small ones under the mantle of forgetful love.

Of these abuses, the most destructive are probably those that arise from the loss of the community's voluntariness. In the first century and in the renewal movements we shall soon be noting, the practice of this discipline was or is at home in a voluntary community whose members have committed themselves to its standards and to its practice, by means of a personal commitment of baptism or confirmation. We can pursue reconciling confrontation because we trust one another and because we asked to be placed under this kind of loving guidance. To do the same things in a nonvoluntary community gives them a quite different meaning; this is where in our culture the word *Puritan* got its bad taste.

Each of these distortions has arisen in history and tends to arise when the label "discipline" is used for the process. Each has let the foundational function of reconciling dialogue slip away from the center of the church's self-understanding. When it is lost, when the image becomes punitive authority rather than reconciliation, then the modern corrective is the backlash of individualism, making self-acceptance a substitute for community: "I'm OK; you be OK!"

It is too little to see in this process an instrument of pastoral care for the individual, though it is that. It is at the same time the mode whereby the community's standards are clarified and, if need be, modified. What in the Mosaic vision was to be done in every locality by "the elders in the gate" was later systematized in the role of the rabbi, who was not so much a preacher or a priest as a steward of the community's moral memory. The ongoing rabbinic process of binding and loosing creates a deposit of precedents and principles known as *halakah,* the "walk" or the "way," the moral tradition. The precise meanings of its guidelines are constantly fine-tuned and updated through the face-to-face exchange about its contemporary applications.

Moral discernment and forgiveness condition and enable one another in complex ways. Admonition presupposes prior discernment; otherwise the criteria for admonition would not be common to both parties. Conversation with reconciling intent is the most powerful way for a community to discover when the rules they have been applying are inadequate, so that they may be modified. Asking whether there has really been an offense helps determine which differences need to be resolved by coming to unanimity by means of dialogue and forgiveness and which call for an agreement to differ. Having experienced forgiveness together enables a community to deliberate in an otherwise inaccessible mode of mutual trust.

Before moving on toward the present, let me summarize the primary components of this mandate; some of them differ from the way our world usually works:

1. Believing men and women are empowered to act in God's name.
2. What the believers do, God is doing, in and through human action.[12]
3. God will not normally do this without human action.
4. If we receive forgiveness, we must give it.
5. This dialogical reconciling process must come first. Only then must we turn to talk of the set of standards that this process enforces. Much Christian debate about moral issues makes the mistake of concentrating on what the standards ought to be rather than on how they are to be discerned and implemented.

Taking seriously this apostolic witness would seem to put us at the mercy of a number of ecclesiastical scarecrows. It gives more authority to the church than does Rome, trusts more to the Holy Spirit than does Pentecostalism, has more respect for the individual than does liberal humanism, makes moral standards more binding than did Puritanism, and is more open to the new situation than was what some called "the new morality" a quarter-century ago. If practiced, it would radically restructure the life of churches. Thus the path to the rediscovery of Christian faithfulness might lead through some positions contemporary Christian "moderates" have been trying to avoid.

Persons concerned for the recovery of the vital moral solidarity of the church have often seen the central importance of binding and loosing. The Reformers of the sixteenth century (Martin Luther, Calvin's teacher Martin Bucer,[13] as well as those later called "Anabaptists"[14]) called this process *Regel Christi*—"The Rule of Christ." They looked to this process to move the Reformation from the university lecture hall and the scholar's office to the life of the parish and the family.

When in September 1524 a circle of dissenting disciples of Huldrych Zwingli,[15] dissatisfied with the slowness with which the Reformation was moving, wrote to the German radical leader Thomas Müntzer,[16] they told him that they admired his courage in denouncing lukewarm religion, but they rejected his advocacy of revolutionary violence. The "Rule of Christ" was the primary mode of reform they exhorted him to use, an alternative to reformation at the command of the prince:

> March forward with the Word and create a Christian church with the help of Christ and His Rule such as we find instituted in Matthew 18 and practiced in the epistles. Press on in earnest with common prayer and fasting, in accord with faith and love, without being commanded and compelled. Then God will help you and your lambs to all purity. . . .[17]

The Anabaptist theologian Balthasar Hubmaier drafted an order of service for fraternal discipline, in addition to arguing throughout his other writings that there could be no renewal of the church without it.[18]

Later movements of renewal, from Pietism and John Wesley to the present, have restored in one way or another this model of loving dialogue. The "classes" and "bands" in Wesley's age performed this function. Wesley prescribed it in his sermon "Cure for Evil Speaking."[19] This process of human interchange combines the mode of reconciling dialogue, the substance of moral discernment, and the authority of divine empowerment. It deserves to be considered one of the sacramental works of the community, although only a few of the reformation traditions came near to saying that. The "catholic" practice carried on by a priest under the heading of "absolution" or "reconciliation" has come to have a much thinner meaning.

If our concern were to be doing a prescribed ritual correctly, that would already be something serious. There would be no reason to make light of the New Testament guidance cited above. But there is much more to it than that. We have here a fundamental anthropological insight into the relationship of conflict and solidarity. To be human is to have differences; to be human wholesomely is to process those differences, not by building up conflicting power claims but by reconciling dialogue. Conflict is socially useful; it forces us to attend to new data from new perspectives. It is useful in interpersonal process; by processing conflict, one learns skills, awareness, trust, and hope. Conflict is useful in intrapersonal dynamics, protecting our concern about guilt and acceptance from being directed inwardly only to our own feelings. The therapy for guilt is forgiveness; the source of self-esteem is another person who takes seriously my restoration to community.

The Christian community has thereby been endowed with the wherewithal for ongoing moral discernment in the face of questions which could not conceivably have been answered substantially ahead of time. Just as a wisely written constitution for an institution or a government provides procedures for amendment and for decision making rather than immutable prescriptions, so the Christian community is equipped not with a code but with decision-making potential.

One early summary statement of this empowerment is the word of Jesus in the Gospel of John: ". . . it is to your advantage that I go away, for if I do not go away, the Advocate will not come to you; but if I go, I will send him to you. . . . When the Spirit of truth comes, he will guide you into all the truth . . ." (16:7, 12).

That promised guide, the Holy Spirit, will operate in the community to make present, for hitherto unforeseen times and places and questions, the meaning of the call of Jesus. It uses a fully human communication process, called by the rabbis "binding and loosing." It has about it elements of what today would be called conflict resolution. It gathers up the resources of human wisdom, the perspectives of several kinds of involvement in different ways of perceiving a question, and loving processes of negotiation, all of this guided and enabled by God's own presence.

Any "social ethic" in the ordinary sense of the term, any *full* system of goals and procedures, which could be adequate to guide the obedience of Christians in one specific situation, would by that very fact have to be out of date or out of place in other situations. When, on the other hand, the guidance we have is constitutional or procedural, any new situation can be met with the resources of valid community process.

The guidance is not only procedural; there are substantial prescriptions as well. We are told to tell the truth, to keep promises, and to care for the needy. Yet the point at which the divine empowerment is crucial has to do not so much with identifying the initial sources of the substantial guidance—the rules to apply—in this or that set of revelatory propositions, as with trusting the Spirit's leading in contextual application.

The conclusion of the Jerusalem conferences of Acts 15:28, "It has seemed good to the Holy Spirit and to us," is presented by the author of Acts as a model for valid process.

The Jesus of Matthew 18 said quite realistically that the discernment process will begin with an important conflict: "If your brother or sister has sinned. . . ." Our modern good manners and our concern to "defang" controversy generally lead us to back away from any element of moral reproach and to say simply that there is a difference of opinion. There may be cases—sometimes—where a question is objectively unresolved without there being any hard feelings or moral reproach, but certainly the generality of psychosocial realism is on the side of Jesus' description. When there is such offense, then a procedure of personal conversation, initially confidential, with the intent of reconciliation, opens the path to a conclusion that will be binding, not only in the immediate social sense of enabling the common life to go on again, but also in the sense of the claimed heavenly ratification of that decision as having been brought about by Christ in our midst.

Before moving from the past to the present, I probably need to attend to one possible misinterpretation to which the above exposition, as well as the later chapters, might be subjected. There are "fundamentalist" and "restorationist" or "primitivist" ways of appealing to the New Testament for normative guidance, as if nothing that happened since the first century matters, or as if the meaning of every text were self-evident without attention to any problems about how to read ancient texts, or as if what the scriptures provide were a rigidly prescriptive and unchanging charter.

I have made none of those assumptions. My concern is not for correct church order for its own sake, as "Campbellite"[20] or Calvinist visions of the "restoration of the New Testament pattern" have sometimes seen it. Yet the shape of the people of God does matter. Medium and message cannot be divorced. The New Testament witness is helpful when read straightforwardly but not legalistically. It enables, as we have already begun to see, paths of change without infidelity, fidelity without rigidity.

I suggest therefore that the high Lutheran thesis is inadequate. It says that the concrete shape of the church does not matter[21] as long as the message of justification by grace alone through faith alone is right. The high Catholic view is wrong, according to which the Bishop of Rome is authorized to promulgate new binding definitions beyond scriptural mandate and according to which absolution is the privilege of a priest. The high liberal Protestant view is wrong, according to which the role of the pope is taken over by a shifting consensus of what literate elites find credible in our time. The high Protestant scholastic view is wrong, according to which an *a priori* affirmation of the revelatory authority of the propositions contained in the canonical books is more important than reading what they say.

What I have been assuming is none of the above, although my straightforward reading of the texts might have made some readers think of me according to one of those stereotypes. Mine might be called a moderately realistic view, taking the texts as they stand, for what they seem to want to say, about the shape of the shared life of the first Christians, holding to a necessary minimum the concern any academic has with getting the preliminaries right. Whether such a mode of reading is intellectually possible will have to be determined by the readers who try it, not by imposing any prior interpretative filter.

This self-conscious attention to theories of interpretation was a detour. It remains to sketch how the practice we have been describing testifies to an understanding of person and community, which extends into the present. The first and simplest meaning would of course be that "the Rule of Christ" as thus described could well regenerate pastoral care and congregational decision making. Where it had been assumed that there is no third way between puritanical legalism and nondirective counseling, it can unite substantial moral concern with redemptive confidential admonition. It can provide a resource for change in personalities and in structures. It can challenge both making forgiveness an automatic routine, as is the danger in some rituals of reconciliation, and making it too dear, as among the second-century Christians who would permit it only once.

The second extension into the present is one specimen of the expectation stated at the outset, namely that the way God wants believers to live together should be a model as well for other social relationships. Conflict resolution is today a socal science and a profession. One can study it; one can be accredited as a practitioner. One can use its theory to analyze successes and failures. One can describe and teach the skills that foster its success. Its rules are not very different from binding and loosing in the New Testament or from "the Rule of Christ" in the Reformation. In a healthy democracy it can function as an alternative to civil litigation or to criminal prosecution.[22] In a chaotic social setting, it can hold things together; under persecution it can strengthen the forces of resistance. Its principles in modern experience thus parallel closely what we have been reading in another language:

a. The process begins at the point of concrete offense, with a real problem.
b. The intention is not punishment but resolution.
c. The frame of reference is a value communally posited as binding the parties.
d. We should assume that the process is not a zero-sum game. The mediator trusts that a solution is available whereby both parties will win; each party affirms the other's rights.
e. The first efforts are made in ways that minimize publicity and threat, and maximize flexibility without risk of shame.
f. The process makes use of a variety of roles and perspectives carried out by competent, caring, yet objective intervenors.
g. The skills and the credibility of intervenors can be validated by experience and accredited by colleagues and clients.
h. The ultimate sanction if negotiations fail is public disavowal of the party refusing reconciliation; what is left is either to let the injustice stand or to see the civil powers intervene in their ordinary way.

In the last decade, we have seen in middle America the rise of a much more narrowly focused ministry rooted in the same gospel mandate. It is called Victim Offender Reconciliation Program, (VORP), a largely church-based ministry intervening, with the authorization of the court, to supplement and sometimes to mitigate or replace the sanctions set for crime by the state.[23]

The victim has been largely ignored in the course of the state's prosecution of crime, and the state's concern for the offender is of course not reparation to the victim but punishment for the crime committed. Trained VORP volunteers negotiate with both parties to enable a voluntary encounter, whereby for the first time the offender can learn firsthand from the victim what it feels like to be burgled or mugged and can project some kind of restitution. Sometimes this reconciliation begins before trial and sentencing; sometimes it comes afterwards. In 1992 about 100 VORP centers were scattered around the United States and Canada. We see here as we shall see elsewhere how the church models for the world what both are called to be and to do.

In sum: To be human is to be in conflict, to offend and to be offended. To be human in the light of the gospel is to face conflict in redemptive dialogue. When we do that, it is God who does it. When we do that, we demonstrate that to process conflict is not merely a palliative strategy for tolerable survival or psychic hygiene, but a mode of truth-finding and community-building. That is true in the gospel; it is also true, *mutatis mutandis*, in the world.

2

Disciples Break Bread Together

In the New Testament passages to which we have given the technical label "words of institution," Jesus said, "Whenever you do this, do it in my memory." What that originally meant may not be as simple as we assume because we have covered it over with centuries of ceremonies and arguments about what the ceremonies mean.

What were they to do in his memory? It *can't* mean "Whenever you celebrate the mass" or "the Lord's Supper": There was then no such thing as "the mass" or "the Lord's Supper."

If we want properly to understand the New Testament,[24] we must invest some effort in disengaging our thought from the fruitless debates of later ages, in particular of the sixteenth century. Those debates dominated the way in which Protestants differed from Roman Catholics and then the way in which Lutherans differed from Calvinists four and a half centuries ago.

Those debates were focused on late-medieval philosophical questions, with which Jesus and his apostles were not concerned. Theologians were concerned in the sixteenth century for a detailed theoretical definition of the meaning of certain special actions and things, called "sacraments," within the special set-apart world of the "religious." The underlying notion—namely the idea that there is a special realm of "religious" reality—so that when you speak special prescribed words, peculiar events happen, was not a biblical idea. It underlies the religion/politics split with which we began in our introduction. It supports one notion of the sacraments as very special religious or ritualistic activities. It had been taken over from paganism by Christians centuries later than the New Testament, when paganism had replaced Judaism as the cultural soil of the Christian movement.

Because that was thought to be the question, Protestants con-demned Catholics, and Calvinists and Lutherans rejected each other, on the basis of abstract debates about the meaning of the bread and the wine—about the definition of what happens to the "emblems" when (and only when) the right words are spoken by a priest.

These medieval questions have kept us away from the simple meaning of the text long enough. *Anachronism* is the name for the mistake people make when they misunderstand something by putting it in the wrong time frame. We make such a mistake when we look in the New Testament for *any* light on those much later eucharistic controversies.

If we had all day, we could work our way back down through one stratum of Christian thought and practice after another, much as an archaeologist works down through a tell. We could ask how and when the straightforward meaning of the Eucharist was overlaid by ritualistic or superstitious notions borrowed from the other religions and philosophical assumptions of the ancient world. We could ask how the synthesis of Christianity and empire beginning in the fourth century had to replace the economic meaning of breaking bread together with something else. The shifts we would find would be analogous to others that took place in the meaning of baptism, which we shall note later.

If we had all of another day, we could also reach back behind the first century to the anthropological meaning of people's eating together. In most cultures, common meals have special mean-ings. We could pursue the specific meanings in the Hebrew heritage of the Passover meal and of the manna in the wilderness. We could review the prophets' predictions about a coming mes-sianic banquet. But for now it will have to suffice to go back to a simple reading of the Gospel text. What then did Jesus mean? What did Jesus mean *then?* What were the first Christians doing when they did it?

Jesus *might* have meant "remember me whenever you cele-brate the Passover," but that is not what his hearers evidently took him to mean. Jews in his day, as in ours, celebrated Passover once a year. The meal just before Jesus' death was in a Passover setting, but what the disciples did in his memory was not a once-a-year event.

What Jesus must have meant, and what the record indicates that his first followers took him to mean, was "whenever you have your common meal." The meal Jesus blessed that evening and claimed as his memorial was their *ordinary* partaking together of food for the body.

That direct connection with ordinary eating together is reinforced by the connection we see in the Gospels between food and the appearances of the risen Lord. In the last chapter of Luke's Gospel, the presence of the resurrected Jesus was correlated with eating. The disciples on the way to Emmaus did not recognize the person who had joined them on the road, talked with them, and reprimanded them for not understanding the scriptures better. They did not identify him until they sat at table and he took over naturally his old role of thanking God for the bread (24:30). Only then did they know who he was. They ran back to Jerusalem to tell the others. There, the other disciples were reticent to accept the report, but they believed it when Jesus appeared again and ate again (vv. 41-43). The same correlation is present in Acts 1:4 and in John 21:9-13.

EATING TOGETHER IN
THE POST-PENTECOST CHURCH

There should be no surprise, then, that the Pentecost account ends with another account of common meals. The disciples' life together is summarized in four activities: Author Luke tells us that they "remained faithful to the apostles' teaching, to fellowship, to the *breaking of bread,* and to the prayers" (2:42) and "they met in their houses for the breaking of bread; they shared their food gladly and generously" (2:46, author's translations). Only because that meal was at the center of their life together could it extend into the formation of economic community: "no one claimed for his own use anything that he had" (4:32). The "common purse" of the Jerusalem church was not a purse: It was a common table. It arose not as the fruit of speculation or discussion about ideal economic relations; it was not something added to what was already going on. The sharing was rather the normal, organic extension from table fellowship. Some of the first Jerusalem believers sold their estates voluntarily (Acts 5 indicates that it was not mandatory) and pooled their goods because in the Lord's presence they ate together, not the other way around.

This common meal was no innovation; it was merely the resumption of the way they had been living together with Jesus for months. As early as Luke 8 there had been references to the way the itinerant band was fed by donations provided for by persons, including some well-to-do women and others, whom Jesus had healed.

The common meal had not been an innovation, but a fulfillment of long-standing expectations when the roving band of Jesus and his disciples shared their bread. The story of manna in the desert had been at the very beginning of the Hebrew liberation experience. Provision for the periodic leveling of the jubilee was at the heart of the Mosaic provisions for making God's ownership of all the land real.[25] When Jesus' cousin and forerunner John was asked by his hearers how to be ready for the coming kingdom, he told them to share their clothing and their food (Luke 3:10,11). Jesus' first temptation in the desert was to make bread. His largest reported audience in the Gospel had been the crowd of thousands whom he fed in the desert, resulting in the clearest affirmation of his messianic calling up to that point.

The centrality of the common meal as what the disciples did together continues into the apostolic age. We read in Acts 6 about the reorganizing of leadership structures in order that the distribution of bread should be equitable. Because the communal meal was so concretely at the center of the community of the disciples, it was natural that this celebration would become the occasion for the next organizational change which Acts reports.

Seven leaders of the "Hellenist"[26] part of the Jerusalem mem-

bership were called to share in leading the community. That
decision initiated the transition from a Palestinian network of
synagogues to a posture of world mission. What that meant for
the future mission of the church and for the meaning of mission
would be worthy of far more attention than we can give it here.
What provoked it, which is our theme here, was the agreed concern that the non-Palestinian widows should be assured their
share in the common meal. That concern was so important that it
demanded a change in leadership patterns, adding to the leadership team persons whom Jesus had not called during his earthly
ministry.

The question of the conditions of table fellowship is what led to
the conference reported in Acts 15, laying the foundation for a
missionary policy that would be free to welcome Gentiles.[27] In
his first letter to the Corinthians, the apostle Paul responds to
requests for guidance which that congregation, soon after he
had founded it, had addressed to him. Most of those requests
for guidance have to do with table fellowship: with meat that
had been offered to idols (Chapters 8 and 10) and with class-
segregated tables (Chapter 11). If their meal failed to reflect the
overcoming of social stratification, Paul told the Corinthians that
the participants would be celebrating their own condemnation
(11:29). In celebrating their fellowship around the table, the early
Christians testified that the messianic age, often pictured as a
banquet, had begun.

In summary, we can discern two simple dimensions of the
practice as it began in the earthly ministry of Jesus among his
disciples. The first is the simple social fact, undeniable in the
record but often not taken to be important, that men and women
left their jobs, homes, and families to constitute with Jesus a new
"family," a community of consumption, in which he exercised
the role of head-of-household. Scholars have sometimes com-
pared the disciples' meals to the kind of gatherings then called
chabourah or "fellowship," where friends would gather regularly
for prayer and food, while remaining in their residential and
vocational settings. That analogy does throw light on the read-

iness of Palestinian society to sustain rapid church growth, but it does not suffice to describe the itinerant disciples' circle. There the household is the model. It is the prerequisite for the meaningfulness of Jesus' words about leaving other loyalties to follow him (Matt. 4:19,20; 10:34-39).[28]

The second dimension of meaning present in the practice at the outset is thanksgiving; the name *Eucharist*, which means simply "giving thanks" in Greek, identifies the meal with its prayer. Every meal in a Jewish household was an act of worship. Presiding at the meals of the disciples' band, Jesus regularly spoke those ancient words of thanksgiving: "Blessed art Thou, God, King of the Universe, by whose goodness we have this bread to share."

FURTHER DIMENSIONS OF THE CELEBRATION

To that basic double meaning (meal fellowship plus thanksgiving) the Gospel accounts add the memory of the celebration of Passover. The Passover too was an act of worship in the form of a meal, celebrated annually, commemorating the flight from Egypt. The "Last Supper" event was in a Passover setting, although the chronological perspectives of the Gospels are not easy to fit together. Mark 14 calls it most simply a Passover meal; John 19 indicates that it rather took place on the day before, called "preparation." In either case the linkage with the Passover season was clearly a part of the report of the celebration. Some of the particular usages, such as the term *cup of blessing* (1 Cor. 10:16) may reflect the Passover celebration.

Through this connection we affirm our loyalty to the entire Hebrew heritage and to the understandings of God as liberator and creator of a people, which the Exodus memory celebrates.

Yet another level of meaning, which we could call on to enrich the picture, is the memory of the feeding of crowds in the desert. Feeding people in the desert had first been proposed to Jesus as a temptation. Later, Jesus did it: He anticipated the promised messianic banquet by feeding thousands, with the not-surprising outcome that they wanted him to be their king.

In the course of such a meal, bearing all the above meanings, Jesus had said, "When you do this, remember me." The report of 1 Corinthians 11 says that these words were spoken in the course of the meal, namely as part of a series of stages, or courses, along the way as the group proceeded through the normal ritual of the family celebration.

THE BASIC ECONOMIC FACT

The level of meaning that matters first for our present purposes, the one that combines with all of the above but came before them and reaches beyond them, is more concrete. It goes deeper than what we call a "ceremony," to what we usually call "economics." What the New Testament is talking about wherever the theme is "breaking bread" is that people actually were sharing with one another their ordinary day-to-day material sustenance.

It is not enough to say merely that in an act of "institution" or symbol-making, independent of ordinary meanings, God or the church would have said, "Let us say that 'bread' stands for daily sustenance." It is not even merely that, as any historian of culture or anthropologist will tell us, in many settings eating together "stands for" values of hospitality and community-formation, said values being distinguishable from the signs that refer to them. It is that bread *is* daily sustenance. Bread eaten together *is* economic sharing. Not merely symbolically, but also in fact, eating together extends to a wider circle the economic solidarity normally obtained in the family. When in most of his post-resurrection appearances Jesus took up again his wonted role of the family head distributing bread (and fish) around his table, he projected into the post-Passion world the common table of the pre-Passion wandering disciple band, whose members had left their prior economic bases to join his movement.

Luke summarizes his account in Acts 4:34: "There was not a needy person among them." He probably meant that as an echo and fulfillment of Deuteronomy 15:4: "There will be . . . no one in need among you." That basic needs are met is a mark of the messianic age.

In short, the Eucharist is an economic act. To do rightly the practice of breaking bread together is a matter of economic ethics.

THE DETOUR OF INTERPRETATION AS SPECIAL "RITUAL"

By interpreting the early Christian meals as set-apart religious rituals, as Christians have been doing since the early Middle Ages, or by trying to interpret them through the narrow focus of a single annual Passover model, we have been enabled to duck their impact for social ethics, first in the church and also in the world. We need to invest extra energy in trying to understand the meaning of simple cultural practices, such as eating together, from culture to culture and century to century. That impact comes clear when we remember that the practice takes off from the family/*chabourah* model of meal-and-prayer gathering which, before Jesus, was a way committed believers shared in one another's needs.

The first embodiment of the economic newness of the kingdom is thus basic economic sharing among the members of the messianic community. But the distinction between an ethic for the church on one hand, derived directly from the content of the gospel as responded to by faith, and on the other hand some other ethic for others, resting on some other base and having some other content, does not follow. The newness of the believing community is the promise of newness on the way for the world. That in the age of the Messiah those in bondage will be freed and the hungry will be fed is also a criterion, though a distant one, for political economics beyond the circle of faith.

It would be too precise if we were to say that the Eucharist commits believers to the advocacy of something like economic democracy or socialism. Socialism as a modern theory has many meanings, too politicized. The most inappropriate use of the term is to describe the corrupt autocratic form of state capitalism which has just collapsed in Eastern Europe.

But it would be too little if we were not to confess that it demands *some* kind of sharing, advocacy, and partisanship in which the poor are privileged, and in which considerations of merit and productivity are subjected to the rule of servanthood. In recent years Christian thought in many traditions has given new attention to the needs or rights of the poor. Roman Catholic social teachings speak of taking the side of the poor. Liberal Protestants speak of social justice in terms of "rights"; others will formulate in other ways their sense of responsibility for basic human needs. What our study adds to this picture is its center; sharing one's own bread is both specimen and symbol of responsibility.

NOT ONLY BREAD BUT ALSO RANK AND STATUS

As we saw already in the witness of 1 Corinthians 11, the Lord's Supper provides ritual leverage for the condemnation of economic segregation. Its context is good news and the work of Christ, which is being experienced already in its first fruits. The grounds for equalization is not (as in much modern Christian concern for economic justice) the vision of an original wholesome order already present in creation[29] and needing only to be restored. It is rather the beginning fulfillment of the promises of the messianic age.[30]

That is why the historical instances of this vision, which have surfaced down through the centuries, have come not from the theologians, not from the bishops, not from the pious landowners, but from the edges of society. Peter Waldo of Lyon, whom some call the first Protestant, left his family's fortune to become an itinerant preacher. His near-contemporary Francis of Assisi left his family's fortune to found a mendicant order. The line runs through the Czech radical Peter Chelcicky in the fifteenth century, condemning in principle the tripartite stratification of feudal society.

A band of nonviolent Anabaptist brethren, expelled from Nikolsburg in Moravia in 1528, joined all of their assets to create the new economic pattern of the church/commune or *Bruderhof*. Gerald Winstanley and the English "Levellers" dug up a field south of London, acting out their rejection of the way in which the "commons" had been taken from them. Down to our own time, Christians taking their discipleship seriously have in various ways found new forms of economic sharing.

These economic radicals down through the centuries did not explicitly unfold their witness from either the theory or the practice of the Eucharist; by their time the development of scholastic eucharistic theology forbade that. But they did know that the poor man Jesus continued to call people to follow him, which meant sharing bread and condemning social stratification. They continued a line that had begun even before Francis and Peter: the *pauperes Christi,* "Christ's poor," who had been called into existence by the Holy Spirit in northern Italy in the eleventh century in reaction to the widespread scandal of "simony" (obtaining church office by paying money).

The same ultimate concern had motivated the older and larger, more official monastic movements. The monk's vow of poverty did not mean destitution: The monastery had property and the monk's life could be comfortable. But no property was *personal,* and beggars were always welcomed. The commitment to work with one's hands (or, in the Franciscan case, to beg) was another expression of economic solidarity. The monastic life remains as a testimony to the commitment to share, even though its forms cannot be a model for our society.

Another substrand of the medieval story was the prohibition of usury, the technical term for lending at interest. This prohibition was carried over by medieval Christianity from the simple words of Moses (Lev. 25:36f, Deut. 23:19, cf. Psalm 15:5) and of Jesus (Luke 6:35), and was kept alive well into the high Middle Ages at the cost of considerable care invested by canon lawyers in defining what was and was not usury. Neither the prohibition of usury nor the prohibition of simony was effective in the long run as a legal cure for economic injustice. What interests us is the fact that in their very persistence on the books and despite their near impotence in terms of enforcement, these two sets of rules testify to the strong reminiscence, up until the Reformation, of the gospel vision of shared poverty, persisting even when the Eucharist had become quite something else.

LEVELING APPLIED TO THE LAND

In his platform proclamation in the synagogue at Nazareth (Luke 4), Jesus cited the reference of Isaiah 61 to "proclaiming the acceptable year of the Lord," probably referring to the Mosaic provisions for the year of Jubilee. Thirty years ago when André Trocmé, French Reformed evangelist, educator, pacifist, pastor, rescuer of Jews,[31] began to elaborate on his realistic vision of the jubilee passage in Luke, it seemed to other interpreters of the New Testament to be a risky hypothesis. Since then it has been a subject of at least three dissertations and various spin-offs in practical social justice ministries. The claim can seriously be argued that the Jesus of Luke 4 did know and did claim what the prophet of Isaiah 61 was promising, namely that in his anointed presence there was beginning a new world whose most dramatic marks would be the forgiving of debts, the redistribution of property, and the freeing of prisoners (most of whom in those days were in prison for debt).

The value of this other strand of the Gospel account is that it protects the "table fellowship" witness from being limited to the level of consumption, without attention to productive resources. The Jubilee is justice on the level of productive capital; everyone should have (which means that every family should have) one's own plot of land. This is an update of the prophetic promise that every household would have its own vine and fig tree (Micah 4:4).

So the reallocation of land ownership every fifty years according to the Mosaic vision is also a forerunner of the sharing of

Jesus' disciples and then of the Jerusalem community. It would be easy, but not fair, to set this witness aside with the test of literalism. The redistribution formulas of Leviticus 25 and Deuteronomy 15 could apply *literally* only among kinship groups that would survive solidly, so that the same extended family could repossess the land they had lost within the last fifty years. It would do nothing to meet the needs of outsiders or of property-less families. It could not be reinstituted after centuries of nonobservance. I doubt that even "Isaiah" meant his proclamation (61:1ff) to refer only to a literal implementation of the Levitical rules. It is even less likely that Jesus did, when he claimed to fulfill that promise (Luke 4:18-21). They both meant to proclaim, using the best imagery available in the Torah, that the anointed one was to bring economic and personal well-being, in whatever form that would need to take in the messianic age.

To include the jubilee message in our vision for the wider world is by no means unrealistic. Every economic order, including capitalism, provides for certain categories of forgiveness and debt amnesty. One form of that in our societies is bankruptcy; another is the low-interest or no-interest loan. Another is public funding of roads, schools, and welfare support. On the international scale, world banking institutions in recent decades have worked out the institutional space for debt amnesty worth billions.

Can a parish or a neighborhood do something of the same kind? Only local discernment can tell which angle of attack on economic discrimination is most fitting, whether counter-cultural model-building, corrective legislation, "voluntary guidelines" for favoring the disadvantaged, ground rules for group interest brokering, advocacy for the underdog, or other solutions.

CHRISTIAN CALLING AND THE "ORDER OF CREATION"

In view of the widespread impact of what is usually called the "Protestant doctrine of vocation," our review will be furthered by a detour at this point. We take note of the insufficiency of that approach in its usual form. That doctrine is a standard way in which Protestant social thought has looked at roles and institutions. It assumes that the Christian will bring to her or his "vocational" role her or his loving intention, integrity, and industriousness, and the modesty resulting from knowing he or she is a forgiven sinner, but that the *content* of one's activity in that "vocation" or "station" or "office," what the person should actually do, does not come from his or her faith in Jesus but from the "order of creation." The institutions in their present shape reveal God's will for the shape of society because God made them that way. That is why the shape of society is called "the order of creation." Each of us is called to live up to the dictates of our "station" or role.

The service of the Christian in his or her secular role must, according to this view, be protected against any too direct carry-over from the Gospel. Some Lutheran theologians call this the *Eigengesetzlichkeit der Kulturgebiete* (the autonomy of each realm of culture), and some conservative Calvinists call it "sphere sovereignty." According to this "order of creation," bankers should accumulate money, not share it, as John the Baptist and Jesus told people to do; that is the meaning of banking as part of the way things just are. Lords should domineer, and soldiers and hangmen should kill, because those are their defined roles in the world. Slaves should remain slaves; women should remain subject; anyone who is under orders should respect the boss.

The natural effect of this vision of authority structures being anchored in the structures of "creation" is of course conservative and patriarchal. Its strongest voices in our time have been the Reformed rulers of South Africa and Northern Ireland. A century and a half ago in the United States, it provided the strongest argument in favor of slavery.

The Gospel answer to this notion is not that there is no such thing as the Christian calling or vocation, but that it is *not* to be distinguished from or contrasted with following Jesus. The notion of an order of creation is not necessarily all wrong, but since sin came into the world we cannot discern which traits of "the way things are" are the way God wants them and which are fallen, disobedient, and oppressive.

If we are to make something of the concept of "vocation" in the light of the Gospel, we must reverse those assumptions. We must undercut the individualism and the pressure to blind conformity of that view of vocation by developing strands of accountability to tie the vocational servant to various constituencies and communities, denying the sovereignty of any sphere over against the Gospel.

This attention to "vocation" was something of a detour just here because it does not apply peculiarly or only to the common meal or to economic matters. It is appealed to all across the board in Christian social ethics. I have lifted it up here because the specimen of banking is an especially pertinent example. The other examples of "corrections," war, patriarchal family patterns, and (longer ago) slavery, which I have just alluded to in parallel, reach beyond our present topic, but they should help to clarify the logic of the difference between the vision of social vocation that we are studying and the traditional "Reformed" one.

If we reclaim the doctrine of vocation in the light of the practices and social vision that we are studying, then the specific ministry of the Christian banker or financier will be to find realistic, technically not utopian ways of implementing jubilee amnesty; there are people doing this. The Christian realtor or developer will find ways to house people according to need; there are people doing this. The Christian judge will open the court system to conflict resolution procedures, and resist the trend toward more and more litigation; this is being done. Technical vocational sphere expertise in each professional area will be needed not to reinforce but to undercut competently the claimed sovereignty of each sphere by planting signs of the new world in the ruins of the old. Baptism is one of those signs, and so is open housing. The Eucharist is one, but so is feeding the hungry. One is not more "real presence" than the other.

3

Baptism and the New Humanity

The apostle Paul had to explain his special missionary policies. As a matter of principle, he made Jews and Gentiles members of the same community, eating and worshiping together.
That policy was being criticized from both sides. In the course of
that argument he wrote to the Corinthians: "If anyone is united
to Christ, there is a new world; everything old has passed away;
see, everything has become new!" (2 Cor. 5:17).[32]

The New English Bible is quite right in translating it this way
("there is a new world"). What is new is the whole world, or
"creation," and not merely the individual (the "creature" as we
are more used to hearing it rendered).[33] Just before that, Paul
had written:

> The love of Christ leaves us no choice . . .
> we are convinced that one has died for all,
> therefore all have died;
> and he died for all, so that those who live might live no
>   longer for themselves . . .
> with us therefore worldly standards have ceased to count in
>   our estimate of anyone;
> even if once they counted in our understanding of Christ,
> they do so now no longer (14-16).

The concrete, social-functional meaning of that statement is
that the inherited social definitions of who each of us is by class
and category are no longer basic. Baptism introduces or initiates
persons into a new people. The distinguishing mark of this
people is that all prior given or chosen identity definitions are
transcended. In this passage Paul is defending the missionary
policies, for which he was being criticized, according to which

28

on principle he makes Jews and Gentiles pray and eat together. What the NEB calls "worldly standards" would more precisely be rendered by "ethnically." The phrase *kata sarka* in verse 16, literally "according to the flesh," means "ethnically."

In a substantially similar way, Paul wrote to the Galatians: "Baptized in Christ, you are clothed in Christ, and there is neither slave nor free, neither male nor female; you are all one in Christ Jesus" (3:27,28 author's translation). That new unity is described elsewhere in the same passage as being "in Christ" (26f), as being "children" or "sons and daughters" (3:26; 4:5-7) and as "new creation" (6:15). When read in the light of Chapter 3, this phrase "new creation" is explicitly a description of what baptism does. The passage spells out Paul's response to the particular pastoral challenge of the situation of the church in Galatia, where the Jew/Gentile transition raised very concretely the question of how ethnic identity would be understood.

The same statement is made in Ephesians 2 where the nouns are *peace* and *new humanity*. "He is himself our peace. Gentiles and Jews, he has made the two one; and in his own body of flesh and blood has broken down the enmity which stood like a dividing wall between them; for he annulled the law with its rules and regulations, so as to create out of the two a single new humanity in himself, thereby making peace" (2:14,15, author's translation).

The wall between Jew and Gentile has been broken down by the death of Christ. The parallel in Galatians (3:28) demonstrates that the fundamental breakthrough at the point of the Jew-Gentile barrier demands and produces breakthroughs of the same type where the barrier is slavery, gender, or class. In the next chapter (Ephesians 3:3) Paul characterizes this message as "my mystery"; that is to say, he claims it as an insight specific to his own ministry.[34] Yet at the same time it is the message which the church by its very existence as a multi-ethnic community "proclaims to the principalities and powers" (3:10, RSV).

In all three epistles, then, in different language, the functional affirmation is the same[35]: Baptism celebrates and effects the merging of the Jewish and the Gentile stories. A people with

the law and a people without, a people walled off from the world
and a people open to it, become a single community, melding
the legacies of both. The several expressions "new humanity,"
"peace," and "new creation," which we have noted, and the contrast between being and knowing "in Christ" (*en christo*) and
being and knowing "ethnically" (*kata sarka*) may well have fig-
ured in the baptismal ritual as equivalent ways of describing the
changed status of one who becomes publicly a confessing be-
liever. This new status is a new kind of social relationship, a
unity that overarches the differences (Jew/Gentile, male/female,
slave/free) that previously had separated people.

The individualism that dominates Western culture falls short of
this vision. According to the dominant perspective, we have
learned to hope that the divisions within humanity can be overcome by means of the summing up of individual parts, whereby
each individual leaves behind the particular identity of the
groups to which he or she belongs, in order to join in the "melting
pot." The melting pot metaphor does not include the separate
identities of each community in the reconciliation as Paul does.

It is not enough to say that each of us is individually born
again and baptized, with the result that all the born-again
individuals are collected in one place, commanded by God to
love one another and plant churches, with no more reason for
discrimination. Paul says more than that; he says that two
peoples, two cultures, two histories have come to flow into one
new humanity, a new creation. The order is thus the reverse of
our modern expectations. There is a new inter-ethnic social reality into which the individual is inducted rather than the social
reality being the sum of the individuals. This new belonging
provokes subjective faith, but it is not the product of the individual's inward believing. It will move history. It will create cultures
and institutions. Yet its truth is not dependent upon those effects
for its verification.

Paul's vision is not first of all an idea that then worked itself
out in a strategy, which then in turn formed a community. It is
rather, as Ephesians 3 said,[36] the lesson he had drawn, after the

fact, from the ministry into which, counter to his own original convictions, he had been providentially drawn.[37]

As Acts describes the two occasions when Paul spoke to Gentiles, first in Lystra (Chapter 14) and then in Athens (Chapter 17), his message was that the God of the Jews was inviting Paul's listeners—Gentiles—into the covenant story that God already had going, that is, the Jewish story. God had done this by virtue of Jesus and the Resurrection."[38] Paul began his exposition by describing the providential order: how all humanity had been made of one blood in order that the different peoples should live together, how providence guides all nations, and how the Jewish preachers of Jesus were "men of like passions" with their Gentile audiences. In other words, a Jewish worldview is here being communicated to non-Jews in their own non-Jewish words. Ethnic pluralism belongs within the order of providence. This proclamation is the backdrop to the messianic announcement. The overcoming of barriers is thus described in Acts in a way substantially parallel to that of the Epistles, though verbally completely different.

The text of 2 Corinthians, with which we began, is more argumentative. Reference to the "new creation" here is part of Paul's defense against his critics. It is because of the newness of the creation that he no longer respects the ethnic or "carnal" distinctions that previously had divided people. The reason those distinctions are gone is the inclusiveness of the cross. Because Christ died for all, that all might live through him, there can be no more discrimination.

The same thing had been said in yet other words, in another set of parallels. When John the Baptist was challenged by the authorities, he said that God makes daughters and sons of Abraham by faith (Matt. 3:9f; Luke 3:8). That was John's reason for accepting all who came to ask for his "baptism of repentance." In those crowds there were unclean Jews (the "tax collectors") and perhaps even Gentiles.[39] Baptism gave them all the same new start.

Jesus said the same thing in John 8, and Paul in Galatians 3. The status of being descended from Abraham is opened to all on the basis not of birth but of faith. To claim Abraham as father was the simplest, strongest way for Jews to state their claim to a special possession "after the flesh"; even this is now opened to others.

Thus the primary narrative meaning of baptism is the new society it creates, by inducting all kinds of people into the same people. The church is (according to the apostolic witness—not in much of its later history) that new society; it is therefore also the model for the world's moving in the same direction.

Later Christian history had to turn several corners in order to open the questions that sacramental theology now debates and that have monopolized attention since then. After the second century, the previously porous border between the church and the Jews was closed so that the lived meaning of the Pauline age was impossible. After the fifth century there were no more outsiders to convert because the whole world had been declared Christian by imperial edict. That made baptism a celebration of birth, reinforcing in-group identity rather than transcending it. Then it was natural that a new theology had to be developed to discuss what the ritual of baptism does to or for the infant who receives it without asking for it.

To answer that, there then had to be developed what we may call a "sacramentalistic" understanding of baptism. This new theology drew on many resources, some of them already well known within the Christian tradition. Others borrowed from Gentile philosophical understandings, such as the notion of an "original" sinfulness linked to being born in a human body. Then the "sacrament" could define in terms of original sin the salvation which the ceremony of a symbolic washing with consecrated water was supposed to mediate to the individual. Within this meaning, there is no reason for the breaking down of barriers between classes of people to be addressed. It does not mean a new age breaking in. There is no clear reason not to do it to a newborn infant who does not ask for it. There is no reason it was wrong to do it coercively to whole tribes in the Middle Ages.

Over against that "sacramentalistic" view, it was natural that in the age we call "Renaissance," other views should develop. Critical rethinking, centering on the place of reason in human nature, developed a new cognitively focused understanding of what "sacraments" should mean, under the heading of cognition or "significance." When Jesus said, for instance, at the Last Supper, "This is my body," the word *is* had to mean "signifies." Likewise baptism properly understood "signifies" a meaning beyond the symbol, which can be stated as knowledge or cognition. This view has come to be named for Huldrych Zwingli, the leader in the reformation of Zurich, Switzerland, beginning in 1519.[40]

Zwinglianism is the tradition that consistently reduces symbolic action to an acted-out message, which can be equally well translated into words (and in fact has to be translated into words so that we can "know what we are doing"). This way of interpreting baptism is most widely represented today by some Baptists, who are in fact radicalized Zwinglians. *If* the idea is that baptism intellectually *signifies* the new birth as an outward symbol representing an inward individual experience, which the one baptized can "confess," then it is obvious logically why we should disavow administering it coercively or to infants. Yet still that "Baptist" view does not naturally imply egalitarianism because what it is trying to explain is a symbolic behavior rather than a social one. It does not make the world new.

On the other hand, we might be able to resurrect what might be called a "sacramental" (rather than either sacramentalistic or Zwinglian) realism. In that understanding, just as we saw in an earlier chapter that breaking bread together *is* an economic act, so baptism *is* the formation of a new people whose newness and togetherness explicitly relativize prior stratifications and classification. Then we need no path, no line of argument, and no arbitrary statement (e.g., "Let us say that this symbol 'x' means . . .)" to get from there to inter-ethnic equality and reconciliation, either in the church or beyond. We start with a ritual act whose first, ordinary meaning is egalitarian.[41] There is no need to ward off its degenerating into a superstitious or magical sacramentalism.[42]

INTERETHNIC INCLUSIVENESS
BEYOND THE CHURCH

Little imagination is needed to see that affirming the oneness
of humanity is one message which by its nature reaches beyond
the church's membership. Affirming trans-ethnic unity will always be fitting for the wider society and will always be needed. It
is, however, possible to make the case for the unity of humanity
on other than Gospel grounds. In our cosmopolitan, humanistic
culture many kinds of arguments for getting along with the
neighbors may be tried. The philosopher of the Stoic tradition
can affirm the dignity of all persons, but for the Stoic, that does
not call for social mixing. Stoic social thought called for each
person to discern, and stay in, his or her place. That approach
does not even guarantee that all humans are "persons." The
modern Reformed theological vision[43] founds its notion of
human rights on a vision of God's taking responsibility for each
individual's dignity, whether by creation[44] or by proclamation;
this does not speak to the ethnic issue.

In our age we know that we need a moral commitment to
human equality reaching beyond ethnic and nationalistic identities, but historically we must acknowledge that modern egalitarianism did not come from the churches. It came mostly from
Enlightenment humanism because it could no longer come
from the missionary meaning of baptism. The churches' debate
about baptism had defined itself into a blind alley, centering on
what the "sacrament" does for the baptized individual.

"Enlightenment" as a label for the sources of modern egalitarianism means partly the Stoic heritage, affirming that each
person has moral dignity, but without making them all equal. It
also meant the appeal to creation, as was already suggested. All
of these sources are present in the background of modern
thought about rights, liberty, and equality.

One modern theological vision, the one we call "Reformed,"
as we saw, founds its criticism of social inequality in a notion of

created nature. As we noted before, the founding document of the United States is a secular version of this approach. It proclaims: "We hold these truths to be self-evident, that all men are created equal, and that they are endowed by their Creator with certain unalienable Rights."

This belief is an important ideological confession of faith, and it was once a noble charter for a revolution, but it is empirically false. "Self-evident" means that people already agree on something without needing to be told or convinced. That is not the case about the equality of all humans. *As people are created,* they are divided among tribes and tongues and peoples and nations. The American South in 1860 and South Africa from 1948 to 1988 are specimens of segregation based on an appeal to creation. Even in Belfast, Ireland, where the segregation is between two kinds of Christians, the theology for it is conservative Calvinism. That is why it is fundamentally different from Paul's equalization message which is rooted not in creation but in redemption.

The equality of all people as they are created certainly is not self-evident. Most people in the world, including most North Americans, do not really believe it. The founding fathers *said,* "All men are created equal," but they *meant* all land-owning white men—excluding all women, black men, Native American men, and poor men.

What it took to begin to free Americanism from racism a century later was not a notion of equality through creation but the good news of redemption. It was strengthened by a sober theological judgment on selfishness and sin, as in the vision of Abraham Lincoln. This vision of a covenant of justice, which the nation had not lived up to, could condemn and call to repentance. Both in the thought of the abolitionists and then in that of Lincoln, it saw equal dignity as a gift of grace, not something with which we are born.

What it took to push emancipation a notch farther yet a century later was the reconciling impact of unmerited suffering in the style of the black Baptist Martin Luther King, Jr.

BAPTISM AND "MISSION"

We shall come back to what baptism means for the social ethical agenda of our time, but first it will be good to pause to recognize briefly some current debates about the missionary practice of baptism. This should verify that our theme is of still broader relevance than what we have thus far been studying. The theological understanding of the missionary enterprise of the church is an openly unfinished agenda in ecumenical theology today. For some, the work that the church is to do is best understood as bringing every listening individual, one at a time, to receiving and responding to new information and an appeal to decide in favor of Jesus. This decision, they believe, will make of that believing individual the "new creature" who was the subject of the traditional mistranslation of 2 Corinthians 5:17, and then that "new person" will be freed from racism as from other sins.

In order to bring about the communication of this appeal, and the resultant individual inner transforming experience, the people who hold this view grant that some social structures and a wider message will, of course, be needed; but those social dimensions are not the message. Once the individual has become new, that newness will have social expressions, they grant, but in an only derivative way. It is important, for this perspective, to distinguish between the "primary" and the "derivative."

On the other side of the debate of the last generation, the Christian mission was held to be not one specific message or ministry, but all kinds of involvement in all that God wants to see done for the whole world. "What God is doing to make the world human" can be discerned, according to that account,[45] by observing and celebrating whatever is going on anywhere by way of liberation and empowerment, whoever does it. These godly processes can be going on and can be discerned and celebrated independent of considerations of personal decision or inwardness or of doctrinal content. There need not be any particular faith content. "Mission" just means that we are sent to join that process and to celebrate it.

For still others, the "mission of the church" should be understood much more realistically, socially (institutionally), as planting viable church communities in every culture, especially where there have been none before. What then if such planting and growth could be facilitated by accepting ethnic isolation and defensiveness because in certain homogeneous cultures people will not forsake their own cultural style?[46] That price in terms of ethical compromise would be worth paying for the sake of church growth.

Widespread current discussions of the Christian mission and of how mission agencies should operate take off from these diversities of understanding. Yet the Pauline understanding is different from all of the above. The messianic age has begun; Paul simply proclaims that fact. He does not seek to bring it about, as if it were for him or his readers to attain. What they are to do is only to announce and celebrate it. Because it has begun, status differences—whether sexual, ritual, ethnic, or economic—are overarched in a new reality.

The truth of this announcement will find an echo with some listeners who will join in the celebration, but as truth it is not dependent upon the echo. The proclaimed truth will have effects, making cultural waves, making history happen, both within the believing community and beyond, but its truth is not dependent on that verification by effects. When heard, the message will change people both inwardly and outwardly, but that change is not the message. The message is that Christ has begun a new phase of world history. The primary characterization of that newness is that now within history there is a group of people whom it is not exaggerating to call a "new world" or a "new humanity." We know the new world has come because its formation breaches the previously followed boundaries that had been fixed by the orders of creation and providence.

We began this chapter by reading three Pauline texts; the beginning of Acts tells the same story in other words. The Book of Acts does not report that the apostles remembered the so-called "Great Commission"[47] and conscientiously set about obeying it.

Nor do we see them thinking about the lost status of individuals whom they had not yet reached. The event of ingathering came first. Only later did the Twelve think about it. Only still later did they "send" someone. The theology to explain the rightness of the ingathering was imposed by the events, which it explained after the fact. The Twelve did not set out to obey the Great Commission; they talked about the risen Lord and they broke bread together in their homes and thus they found themselves together first with Hellenized Jews and then even with Gentiles. *Then* a theology had to be unfolded to make sense of the ingathering, and adjustments in church order had to be made to affirm and guide it. The action of mission was prior to theory about it.

This observation might provide some guidance within the currently lively debates about "church growth" and cultural homogeneity.[48] Should the missionary message be modified, for instance, by not making an issue of social justice, if that would enable people to accept it more easily? Can the social sciences be appealed to in order to guide the choice of the target audience most likely to listen and the formulation of the message most likely to be accepted?[49] The argument is usually about whether "growth" should be described qualitatively or quantitatively or in some other way.

As is the case with many lively debates, the question is wrongly stated. We do not have to choose between a message for the inward person followed by social implications, on one side, and on the other side a social program. The first-century story we are watching certainly does indicate that it is part of the Gospel message to take account of ethnic and cultural considerations. The importance of ethnic considerations is qualitative, even definitional, consisting in the fact that the bounds of culture's homogeneous groupings are overcome, not ratified. If reconciliation between peoples and cultures is not happening, the Gospel's truth is not being confirmed in that place.

Our next, broader question is how this message reaches beyond the faith community to the world. Can this quality of the church as "new creation" aid in enabling Christians to find a social witness to address to the old creation, to what John calls "the world"? We assumed a few pages ago, when contrasting Paul's message with Jefferson's, that such an extension was logically congenial, but is it mandatory? Is it legitimate? This message does happen to be the one point at which there is explicit apostolic reference to a proclamation "to the powers" that dominate the fallen creation, namely in Ephesians 3:10.[50] Why are "the powers" the audience to whom the creation of the new humanity constitutes a proclamation? Is it not because, as guardians of the created order in its fallenness, they have a vested interest in keeping peoples separate and alienated from one another?

The apostolic proclamation is thus not a theory either about creation or about the dignity of the individual. Rather than speaking politely and generically about renewal or wholeness, it is an explanation of the meaning of certain social events. It announces and explicates the fact that because of the death of Jesus, whom we confess as Messiah, outsiders have got in on our story. Abraham has more sons and daughters than only his biological descendants: Even the language of family is broken open to adopt the outsider. This event is historically founded in the deeds that God has done, not in some previously valid intellectual awareness about what human nature always was. That is why the question had come to Paul in Athens in the first place. The Athenians thought that Paul was announcing two new deities, Jesus and resurrection (see Endnotes, No. 38). It was by *naming* the risen Jesus that Paul ended his description of the providential plurality of peoples (17:30-32). In other words, in this proclamation of universality there is no backing away from the particularity of the Jesus story, no soft-pedaling of the missionary imperative.

But if now we affirm that there is a distinctly Christian and, in fact, evangelical basis for announcing to the whole world the rejection of all ethnic, sexual, and class discrimination, will this not make it look as if we in the churches were merely tagging along behind the world, trying to use words of our own to say something that the world taught us needed saying? The question is important. It is clear that from the time of Constantine until a century ago, the mainline Christian understanding on these matters did in fact point in the opposite direction. Christian authorities claimed on the grounds of creation and providence that peoples, nations, and classes should stay apart, that men should rule over women, and that Europeans should rule the globe.

That left it to the Enlightenment, the intellectual culture of doubt that gained strength in the eighteenth century, to make the case for equal dignity. Thus it can very well seem now that the churches' joining the equality movement has about it an element of Johnny-come-lately, trying to catch up with a bandwagon. That only reinforces the importance of our clarifying that the New Testament has its own grounds for its own egalitarian witness, differently shaped from that of the Enlightenment, older and more deeply rooted, even though it has been lost and betrayed for centuries.

The original Christian equality message, to sum up, was rooted in the work of Christ, not in creation or providence. It was integrally part of the very definition of the meaning of the cross (as we saw especially in Ephesians 2 and 3), not merely a derivative from or an implication of the Christian's change of heart or mind. It was visible in the concrete bodily form of people who changed their dietary patterns so that they could eat with each other. That vision was soon lost when the Hellenization and Romanization of the churches went so far (in some places by the middle of the second century, in others much later) as to abandon the open interface with Judaism and to accept the beginnings of Christian anti-Judaism. From then on the only unity message is the weak kind of equal-but-separate statement, which does not demand eating at one table and does not condemn empire or patriarchy.

OTHER DIMENSIONS OF
THE POLITICS OF BAPTISM

Inter-ethnic inclusiveness has been our theme thus far, but baptism has other "political" dimensions as well that reach into the world around us. Before Paul and the new humanity, even before Jesus, baptism also meant repentance and cleansing. It meant "You can leave your past behind." John's annunciation of the kingdom enabled his hearers to begin a new life. Does this too have a secular analog? What now does it mean to others for Christians to say, "You can change"?

One of the standard challenges of social ethics is the temptation to borrow from the social "sciences" a model of what it means to be scientific, which in turn had been borrowed from the natural sciences. That model assumes the fixity of character and therefore promotes quasi-mechanical understandings of psychic and social causation. Within this context we are then predisposed toward models of social process that box the offender or the adversary into his or her past path.

The gospel says, however, and baptism celebrates that a new life is possible. At least in analogical ways, the category of repentance can be communicated beyond the church. For one example, the power of nonviolence is that it gives operational shape to our permanent readiness to see our adversary as able to change. Gandhi learned this by reading Tolstoy, although he had not encountered it among the Christians he knew well. As we saw above, under another heading, the goal of nonviolent action is not the destruction or even the repression of the adversary, but his or her conversion. Nonviolent techniques in the struggle for civil rights do much to celebrate the dignity of the downtrodden, without which such techniques would not "work." Yet their uniqueness is greatest at the point of their protecting the dignity of the adversary. They appeal to the conscience of the oppressor. They refuse to deal with the oppressor in terms of the oppressor's past and past or present guilt.

If nonviolence were only an appeal to the guilt of the beneficiaries of injustice, then its appropriateness and probably some of its pragmatic effectiveness would be dependent on the presence of guilt feelings on the part of those whom one seeks to influence. Some racists feel less guilty than others. If the meaning of the civil rights struggle or of any nonviolent action was that it could exploit the guilt feelings of the white middle class, then we might have less to say to those who feel less guilt. There might be nothing at all to say to those who feel righteous about their oppressive role.

If, on the other hand, Christian baptism proclaims and celebrates that change in identity, understanding, and behavior (what the apostles call "repentance") is possible for all, then whether people feel guilt may not be so important. What is important is the clarity of the call to reconciliation, to which the nonviolent provocation calls the adversary. It is possible for all because it has already been celebrated in Christian baptism by some of us.

I have been describing nonviolent conflict here as an analog to the call to conversion. This is the way such activities have functioned, for example, at the edge of the constitutional order in the campaigns of Gandhi or King. The same witness must apply as well closer to the middle range of social process, in conflict management within institutions, and in exercising the skills of conflict resolution. Within the social sciences in the last generation, there has grown up a broad dissatisfaction with the "equilibrium" models that sociologists used to use for understanding a society in favor of patterns that observe conflict and change. To approach any conflict under the axiom that the adversary shares the same human dignity that God has ascribed to us without any merit on our part is to bring to the management of that conflict a powerful *a priori* ground, founded in baptism, for expecting redemptive change.

BAPTISM AND RELIGIOUS LIBERTY

Baptism has yet a third implication for social structures, an obvious one, to which I have given less attention only because we tend (perhaps wrongly) to assume that it is already taken care of in our English-speaking societies.

We have seen that the practice of baptism in the early church meant the reconciliation of two cultures and peoples. What baptism means for the convert in relation to a pluralistic society, however, is the person's free choice to join a movement in response to having heard a message that invites her or him to become a member. The voluntariness of joining was not our first concern until now, but in any society where some specific religious stance is strong, it becomes important.

A civil order ought to give room for free religious decision and adhesion, as ours officially does. In many parts of the world, authentic religious liberty is still not secure. That it is secure in our own land is an assumption that was made too easily during the last century, when its practical meaning was only the freedom to choose one's own kind of respectable Protestantism.

Rough edges still exist in the Anglo-Saxon cultures concerning the connection between religious liberty and the freedom of nonreligious speech, concerning the rights of authoritarian and obscurantist faiths, concerning whether religious liberty must include or exclude tax exemption for church agencies, and concerning the extent to which majorities may properly dominate the schools or the media.[51] I leave these matters without adequate treatment here because, in contrast to the other two dimensions of the meaning of baptism, one may hope that their pertinence and their complexity are already well known; yet it is not really assured that our society will defend the rights of real dissent.

A COMMON PATTERN BEGINS TO FORM

Thus far we have surveyed three practices of the early church, asking in each case about its contribution to mission and politics. Now we can look back across the ground we have covered and hazard a first trial balance. Fraternal admonition, the multiplicity of ministries, and baptism are utterly independent of one another in their form as in their subject matter. They come from separate strata of the New Testament, each with its own vocabulary. Yet there is a far-reaching formal commonality arising from our observations; it authorizes us to make a first step toward what logic calls "induction."

Let us begin to pull these threads together already in this third chapter in order to be able to carry this sense of the logical parallelism with us as we go along into the next two subjects.

A. Of all three practices it is formally said in the New Testament that when humans do it, God is doing it. This would justify our using the word *sacrament* if the term had not been burdened by mechanical or magical misreadings through the centuries. I have sometimes proposed to try to retrieve the term and have tried to do so above, distinguishing between "sacramental" and "sacramentalistic," but we are not always able to commend to others a corrected use of traditional terms.

B. Of all three practices it is the case that the practices are ordinary human behavior. To reconcile through dialogue, to share bread with one another, or to fuse two cultural histories into one new shared community are not mysterious. No esoteric insight is needed for them to make sense. A social scientist could watch them happening. There are no necessary correct holy words to make the rites "right"; no special chapter titled "theology of sacraments" is needed to describe what is going on.

C. Of all three practices, it is further the case that doing them is what makes a group what it is. To study them is the domain not of semantics, aesthetics, or dogmatics, but of sociology. All three practices are public, accessible beyond the faith community. One can extrapolate each of them into a secular or a pluralistic frame of reference. (A major preoccupation of one contemporary school of academic theologians is how we can communicate the Christian message to a public that no longer is familiar with the jargon of the church. That may be a real problem in some areas of specific in-group thought, but it obviously does not apply here. None of these practices is ritualistic or religious or esoteric in the regular, narrower sense of those terms.)

D. All three of these practices are described in the New Testament as derived from the work of Jesus Christ. Binding and loosing is a direct command of the earthly Jesus according to the account of Matthew 18 and Luke 17 and of the risen Lord according to John 20. The breaking of bread, following instructions Jesus is recorded as giving, celebrates the death of Jesus and his expected return. The breaking down of the wall of separation in Ephesians 2 and the making of the new creation in 2 Corinthians 5 are brought about by the death of Christ. Baptism celebrates the status called "being in Christ," brought about by the cross. These practices are not, in the New Testament—as many would prefer—preceded by or dependent upon some wider, deeper, or more general knowledge of either God or the world. Yet this closeness to Jesus does not do without the Holy Spirit (expressly invoked in John 20:22) or the Father ("what you bind is bound in heaven").

This reminds us of a concern that is widespread in modern theology (present in some ancient theologies as well) to get loose from a too-close loyalty to the Jesus of the New Testament. Sometimes people mean by this that they want to affirm the superiority of creation over redemption. Sometimes (as recently with Helmut Richard Niebuhr[52]) they mean to claim a priority for "God" as Father or as Trinity over against too much concentration on the Son. Sometimes this concern takes the shape of contrasting the Epistles with the Gospels or Jesus with Paul; sometimes the contrast is between the cosmic Christ and the historical one.[53]

There would be occasion here for a deeply abstract debate concerning theological method, about the relationship be-

tween the Jesus of the New Testament and other higher or
deeper kinds of claims to know God. This would merit a se-
mester's academic study, but *it does not belong here.* It is not
pertinent to these texts or to these practices. The nuances
that might thus be identified would give no ground for
changing what we think of our five Gospel practices. There is
no need for an apologetic front porch or for "epistemological
prolegomena"[54] to enable or validate or assure the message's
meaningfulness.

E. It is true of all three practices that they have a social meaning at the outset. None begins with a statement about inward
experience or with conceptual information or illumination
from which the social meaning needs to be derived indi-
rectly. Each activity is at the outset—by its nature, not only
by implication—social, practical, and public. By its very
nature, without any complex argumentative bridge being
needed either to explain or to justify, these practices can be
prototypes for what others can do in the wider world. Beyond
the faith community it is possible to resolve conflicts and
make decisions by conversation, to feed the hungry, and to
build interethnic community by inclusion. They are not only
political in that they describe the church as a body with
a concrete social shape; they are also political in the wider
sense that they can be commended to any society as a
healthy way to organize.

F. It is true of all three practices that they constitute procedural
guidelines. They have to do more with a style of approaching
any question than with particular moral choices. They foster
flexibility and readiness to approach any new challenge. That
frees them from bondage to any one cultural setting; it frees
them for evangelical integration into any new missionary
context. They are all good news, all marks of the new world's
having begun.

4

The Fullness of Christ

This chapter addresses a part of the New Testament witness we have often greeted from afar without really understanding it; it would throw light on a set of problems about roles, relationships, professions, and skills, concerning which we are often at odds. Rather than attempt first to name and analyze the present questions, let us begin again with the apostolic witness itself.

The Paul of Ephesians uses the term *the fullness of Christ* to describe a new mode of group relationships, in which every member of a body has a distinctly identifiable, divinely validated and empowered role.

> His gifts were that some should be apostles, some prophets, some evangelists, some pastors and teachers, . . . for building up the body of Christ . . . until we all attain to the unity of the faith and of the knowledge of the Son of God . . . to the measure of the stature of the fullness of Christ (Eph. 4:11-13, RSV).[55]

We may in fact owe to Paul the currency of the metaphor "body," which is so widely used in our language to describe a social group.

The Paul of 1 Corinthians says literally that *every* member is the bearer of such a "manifestation of the Spirit for the common good" (1 Cor. 12:7).[56] He prescribes quite detailed guidelines, which run counter to our intuitions and our habits, for how this vision of the dignity of every part of the organism should lead his readers to ascribe the greater value to the less honored members.

The Paul of Romans instructs his readers about their ability

and their duty to think of themselves in such a way as to conform
to the grace that God has given to each of them (12:6). When he
writes "according to the measure of faith that God has assigned"
(12:3), he does not mean that some people have been dealt out a
lot of faith or grace and some only a little. "Measure" is not like a
yardstick, to evaluate quantitatively, some people's enablement
being bigger than that of others. "Measure" here is like a dipper
which apportions to each person at table his or her own share.

Paul tells his readers to see all of this diversity of enablements
as a specific working of God the Spirit, present in, with, and under a particular pattern of social process. The same way of speaking also appears in 1 Peter (4:9ff). This indicates that the entire
thought pattern is not original with Paul or peculiar to him. It was
more widely the possession of the early Christian communities,
although it is Paul who spells it out most fully for us.

When Paul was writing, this pattern for the definition of roles
in the group differed profoundly from the patterns that already
were present in his world, just as it differs profoundly from our
own. Sharing roles was not a culturally available social model.
His advice also differs from most of what later Christian history
has done with the notions of "charisma" and "ministry," or with
the notion of "body." As we go on with the description, the novelty of Paul's point will be more understandable if we look at the
contrast with today's dominant assumptions. These assumptions take different shapes in different denominations, but their
outlines are similar. According to this standard account, a very
few persons—one or, at the most, two or three in a congregation
or parish—has the special role of "minister." Only this especially qualified person can do the special thing that makes the
church what it is supposed to be.[57]

NOT MERE HUMAN POTENTIAL: A MIRACLE

According to the image of Psalm 68, which Paul claims as a
metaphor in Ephesians 4, the distribution of gifts to all is a part
of the victory of Christ. Taken alone, this image of the body,

with its several members organically coordinated, could have been exploited as a very conservative social image, describing the status quo with its several role relationships as being the same as revelation. It has in fact often been used that way. But these verses were addressed to the church at Ephesus just after the strong accent of the preceding chapters upon the non-natural quality of their unity, in no way taken for granted or self-evident.

This complementarity of many gifts is not described as living out a code already present in the nature of things, such as the way our genes bear a pattern for our physical body to grow into. Paul rather calls it "making your calling sure," consolidating the gift just received from the ascending Lord and living up to a direction we have just been shown.

Probably one of the reasons modern Protestants have difficulty in taking seriously the novelty of the doctrine of the multiplicity of gifts is that we think we already understand it. We equate it with commercial and industrial models of cooperation and teamwork about which we already know.[58] The apostle, on the other hand, says that it had not already existed or functioned before. It rather had to be achieved by Christ; it is a part of the triumphal procession of YHWH/Adonai leading captives in his train and sharing with his people the booty of his victory.

There may be some long-range cultural-historical sense in which this notion of the gifted dignity of each person is at the root of Western individualism. The value of the individual is part of the gospel; we need not disavow paternity. Yet from our end of the evolution of the culture of individualism, we must discern that the differences are greater than the similarities. The hand of the body or the eye is in no sense "individual." It is unique and irreplaceable, yet it can possess and exercise its own dignity, its own life and role, only in its bondedness with the other members. It can be crippled for no fault of its own when some other part of the body suffers.

Although Paul's argument is rooted in the Good News about the work of Christ and his appeal is pastoral, his vision of human dignity can nonetheless be translated into terms outsiders can understand in order to deal with role relationships in groups other than the church. Every human being, Christian or not, is less than he or she could and ought to be if not part of a body in organic interdependence with many peers. That vision of organic interdependence translates into social ethics, in ways that cannot be reduced either to individualism plus social contract on one hand or to corporatism and subsidiarity[59] on the other, although it will support some of the criticisms that each of those theoretical systems directs against the others.

KEEPING THE BODY TOGETHER

The first situational challenge that led to the use of body imagery by Paul was the privilege claimed by a few Christians in Corinth who believed that their ministry was more "spiritual" than that of other members. Paul in response does not deny the spirit-driven quality of their ministries, but he surrounds his recognition of them with three very serious qualifications:

a. He says that *every member* of the body has been given *some* gift by the same Holy Spirit and that all of the gifts are of equal dignity. Thus each bearer of any gift is called, first of all, to reciprocal recognition of all the others, giving "special honor to the less comely members."

b. He reminds the Corinthians that from the point of view of the health of the community, despite the intrinsic equal dignity of all gifts, there are some values that take priority over others within the deliberative assemblies of the *ecclesia*.[60] One of those is rational, edifying communication, which he calls "prophecy." Another is the orderly arrangement of the communication process, including the duty to listen critically to one another.

c. Paul changes the tone of the conversation by changing the language. It would seem that the label "spiritual" (*pneu-*

matic in Greek), which he uses as if its meaning were clear, was already being used as a designation by some people to describe their own persons and their functions, to the exclusion of others. Paul replaced the word *spirit* with *gift* (*charisma*, from which we get *charismatic*) meaning grace-given. He thus moved the accent from the claim an individual would make to possess the spirit uniquely, to the acknowledgment that whatever one's role is, it has been given by the Spirit, and is thereby dependent or derivative, not a reason for pride.

Paul was thus offering a corrective in the face of the unbridled enthusiasm which was in that setting a potential danger of disorder. Soon, however, another kind of function in the church came to be overvalued, namely that kind of role that was accredited by succession, by rituals of installation, or by the possession of a tradition. This kind of role was generally held by only one person or a very few. It usually was held by a man and defined in terms of some power he held over others.

THE SAME VISION IN A DIFFERENT PLACE

Thus the critical corrective impact of Paul's message, which has been needed most of the time since then, is not, as it was in Corinth, to relativize self-validating enthusiasm. It would rather be now that we should renew the underlying understanding of the Spirit's work, which created the vitality that then needed to be called to order. Paul *first* said, "Every one has a gift"; *then* he said, "Let everything be orderly." We too need the first truth, as Good News, before the second. In the name of the first truth we need to challenge the concentration of authority in the hands of office-bearers accredited on institutional grounds. To do so we need to renew the original vitality that Paul had needed to rein in only after it began to overreach itself. Thus it has occurred repeatedly through the centuries, that one impact of biblically oriented renewal has been to reopen the notion of charisma, rediscovering patterns of ministry in addition to or over against the male monarchical ones that had settled in over the years.

Our understanding of this message has been ill-served by developments in modern language usage, which employ Paul's own words in a way contrary to the thrust of his teaching. One is the use of the term *charisma* borrowed widely from the German sociologist Max Weber. Weber called one kind of centralized leadership "charismatic." By this he designated the way in which, especially in a new movement, a powerful central leader can come to prominence because of some special capacity he or she has to gain the trust of many followers. Weber thereby gave to the word *charisma* a meaning diametrically opposite to the pastoral intention Paul had when introducing it. Paul meant the term (which some scholars think he himself may have invented) in order to downplay the spectacular and powerful, calling for modesty, since each such capacity or role is a *gift*. Weber, on the other hand, used the term to describe functions whose authority is spectacular or imposing, self-authenticating. This misunderstanding became all the worse when it was borrowed in communication and media theory to describe someone who is especially photogenic or short on modesty or stage fright.

A second confusing usage is the choice of the label *charismatic* to describe one particular model of personal piety and church renewal, which has been very effective during the last thirty years. Some Christians are "charismatic" and others are not, according to this usage. Sometimes this special usage has been the choice of the people themselves; sometimes it has been chosen by journalists, historians, and critics outside the movement. Thus the word again serves to label a special tendency within the church, a fraction or a caucus, to the exclusion of other perspectives or other persons, thus again making of the word just the opposite of what Paul intended.

Yet another confusion is the modern usage of *gift* or *giftedness* as a designation for exceptional innate capacities or for secular vocation. The gifts Paul describes are not something persons can possess independently of the salvation story or of

Jesus' Lordship. They are not like perfect pitch or exceptional muscular coordination or a knack for learning language. They are not innate (though some of them may correlate with physiological endowment).

Nor are they like the social station (called "office" or "vocation" in Reformation social theory) where one finds oneself in the secular economy. The lists of roles in the Pauline texts (Romans 12; two in 1 Corinthians 12, a briefer one in Ephesians 4)[61] describe functions within the gathered *ecclesia:* apostle, prophet, teacher, elder. They do not list social roles such as "butcher, baker, candlestickmaker" or "rich man, poor man, beggarman, thief, doctor, lawyer, merchant chief." In the sixteenth century, the importance of what the Reformers called "lay vocation," namely socioeconomic roles such as butcher, baker, and candlestickmaker, was properly emphasized for good reasons having to do with the renewal of the Christian life, but with a different focus and for reasons different from our present concern. (See pp. 25ff. above.) That retrieval of the honor of the secular vocation was a needed correction for the overvaluing of clerical and monastic ministries, but it was not based upon this Pauline message. It was on a different subject. Professional specialization is a good thing, but the diversity of charismatically empowered roles is not the same as professional specialization. Becoming recognized as a profession gives independent dignity to a function standing alone, accredited and salaried in its own dignity. Paul's metaphor, on the other hand, accentuates reciprocal accountability and interdependence.

Elsewhere in Western cultural history, there are body images that give special honor to one of the members of the body as its head, and thereby point toward hierarchical visions of society. In past Protestant experience, that has often been linked with the notion of vocation we have just been considering and with the notion that God's will for social structures is revealed "by creation" in the way those structures are. Paul's metaphor, on the other hand, relativizes hierarchy because Christ, not one of the other members, is the head. In 1 Corinthians 14 there is a certain functional hierarchy, we noted, in that understandable prophecy is preferable, if one must choose, to unintelligible speaking in tongues; but Paul said he did not want his readers to have to choose. Both were valid; he practiced both and wanted others to do so.

There is a certain chronological priority belonging to the apostles and prophets, who are the link to the communities' memory, but the apostles will die out and the prophets are to be subject to the communities. There is a kind of procedural priority to the functions of elder-moderator and elder-teacher, but the teaching office is warned against, because of the special temptations of playing with words.[62] The eldership, in the early church as in the synagogue, seems to have been plural, shared with a team of colleagues, a role for which one is not qualified without long and successful experience in family life. Thus the ultimate impact of Paul's use of body image is clearly and consistently antihierarchical.

In our century, in a way that differs from the first or the sixteenth, there is no need to explain the nature of a call for role diversity; what is needed today is to be clear about its grounds. Especially Paul's hope needs to be protected against wrongly negative interpretations of what he wanted. Paul does not call for a participatory community style because of a post-enlightenment conviction about the absolute dignity of every person. He does not reject domination because of a belief that the government, the marketplace, or the factory was created by a contract of freely negotiated individuals in order to maximize the selfish interest of each and protect them against the threat of anarchy. He does not believe that every individual is predominantly good and that therefore the summation of the individual's interests and inclinations will make the best of all societies. He is not opposed to the domination of clergy and priest because he thinks that every individual should be saved according to his or her own conscience. He does not "reject leadership" on the grounds of a countercultural suspicion of all authority or because of the confidence that things will take care of themselves if all structures collapse. He rather confesses, even proclaims, that in the midst of a fallen world the grace of God has apportioned to every one, without merit, a renewed potential for dignity in complementarity. This is not an anti-structural stance; it is the affirmation of a structure analogous to the human organism. God has done this not by making everyone the same, but by empowering each member differently although equally.

THE POWERFUL ALTERNATIVE

I said at the outset that Paul's message was "counter-intuitive and counter-traditional"; that needs to be said more strongly. There is a far-reaching tendency in all cultures and societies, represented in religions of all kinds, whether that of an African village or that of an ancient Mesopotamian empire. In all traditional cultures the priest, the shaman, the professional purveyor of access to the divine, holds the monopoly of those very special goods which people need in the high or the low points of their lives. Sometimes the specialist is qualified by inheritance, sometimes by special initiatory ceremonies or training, sometimes by control of a holy place. The specialist may solemnize the turning points of the calendar, or of the individual life cycle, or of the weather. The ceremony, which only the priest or rarely a priestess can perform, is the only way to please the gods and assure the fertility of one's family and fields and flocks or the courage of one's warriors or the proper rhythm of sun and rain. Despite these enormous differences in that for which the holy person is essential, the underlying assumption is always there. The special role of the professional religionist is part of the fallen nature of things, a universal anthropological constant[63] underlying the great varieties of form just listed.

Already in ancient Israel, God acted to relativize the centrality of the priestly specialist. Abraham was not a priest; he took his sacrifice to Melchizedek. Moses was not a priest; he let his brother, Aaron, and then the Levites do those rituals. On the advice of his father-in-law, Moses farmed out to others the role of adjudicating conflicts (Exodus 18). In Numbers 11 at YHWH's instruction Moses called seventy men to share with him the Spirit's empowerment: "Would that all the Lord's people were prophets!" (11:29).

Throughout the Israelite story, the activities of prophets, judges, and "the elders in the gate" relativized the centrality of the ritual life although they still honored it. After the end of kingship and the loss of the Jerusalem temple, Jewry survived not by creating a surrogate for the Temple so as to keep using the priesthood, but by inventing a new role, that of the rabbi, steward of the Torah, and a new social instrument, the synagogue, formed of any ten households, with no religious specialist needed in their midst at all.

By the time of Jesus, the Temple with its priesthood had been restored, but he relativized it again. He formed a movement out of fishermen, zealots, and publicans—and women—sending seventy of them (the same number as Moses) out across the countryside. That set the stage for the qualitatively new impact of the Christian movement, as interpreted in the Pauline texts we have been reading. Among the first Christians at Jerusalem were some priests who continued to take their turns at officiating in the Temple, but they had no priestly role in the messianic synagogues because there was no sacrificial worship there. The specialized purveyor of access to the divine is out of work since Pentecost.[64]

Sometimes the early Christians said they were all priests; sometimes they said that the priesthood was done away with. The concrete social meanings of the two statements, though verbally opposite, were the same. All members of the body alike are Spirit-empowered. The monopoly of the sacrificial celebration that enables and delimits human access to the divine is swept away. The priestly person as the primary agent of access to the divine is swept away with the special ceremonies. Jesus was the last sacrifice and thus he was also the last priest.[65] The antipriestly impact of this change, although expressed emphatically in the Pauline writings and in Hebrews, is one of the dimensions of redemption least noted and least honored in Christian history since then.

Soon, as we have already seen, the sweeping Pauline vision was lost. Because no central authority existed in the early churches,[66] it probably never generally won out in the first place. The notion that there are several ministries remained for a while—deacon and deaconess, lector, exorcist—but the conviction that *every* member of the body is charismatically empowered for a nameable role was soon lost. We need not ask whether the "blame" for this loss should be assigned to a resurgence of patriarchal social habits or to the assimilation of pagan notions of sacrificial cult or to certain threats of disorder which someone felt a need to ward off or to the domination of later generations by the habits of churches which had never heard or accepted the Pauline message in the first place. We often forget that what we call the New Testament canon was not that for two centuries.[67]

Still later, the restored monopoly of the priestly role was reinforced by its alliance with the sacral notion of kingship, renewed in the fourth century by Constantine.

In any case, Paul's vision has yet to be consciously and consistently lived out. In various renewal movements over the centuries there has been *some* sense of lay empowerment and decentralized accountable leadership, but it seldom lasts long. It is seldom thought through as an intentional part of the reformation project. Although the Friends, the Plymouth Brethren, and the Salvation Army have come closer than most Protestants to relativizing the priestly monopoly and validating varied ministries, even they did not set out to realize what Paul had written about. It happened to them, as they were being led by the Spirit on other fronts, that they found God empowering nonclergy, including women, and they honored these gifts, but they did not generalize. Something of this is happening again today in the "base communities" of Latin America, but again without being programmatically intended.

Although Paul's warrant for his exhortation is derived from the order of redemption, his vision of complementary functions, working together after the model of the several members of the human organism, is applicable to any organization with complex tasks. The modern notions of teamwork, which I argued above are not the source of Paul's vision, are in fact reflections or spin-offs from it. It enables the detailed analysis of the several functional components of any task, so that each can be most appropriately discharged. It enables the factory system, the research team, the university, and the city. It explains why factories and businesses where every worker participates in policy making and quality control can make better automobiles or sell more software than those whose organization is vertical.

OUR THEME IN ITS CONTEXT

We have now looked at four practices commanded and, to some degree, practiced in the early churches. As distinct from the others, this specimen of prescribed social process does not fall within what ordinarily is called worship. Even less would we ordinarily speak of it as liturgy. Yet why should it not be so designated?

Later some vestiges of the notion of "charisma" were built into the medieval sacramental system, but with the loss of the heart of the matter. The "sacrament of orders," for instance, developed in a way that recognized the divine empowerment of only a few, all of them men, at the price of excluding the ministries of all other believers, thereby falling back into the notion of the religious specialist, which—according to Paul—Pentecost had brought to an end, and into the image of the set-apart priesthood as characterizing church leadership.

Similarly, the medieval "sacrament of penance" or of absolution carried over from the gospel vision the component of mediating the remission of guilt—in other words, a counterpart to "binding and loosing"—but disconnected it from the pastoral responsibility of every member for the concrete obedience of every brother or sister, tying it instead to the rare privilege of the priestly confessor who alone can absolve. It was disconnected as well from the process of moral discernment because the authority for moral guidance (moral theology, catechesis) was entrusted to a different member of the sacerdotal hierarchy than the authority to forgive.

In ways not very different from the loss of "binding and loosing," the full meaning of breaking bread together and the full meaning of baptism as constituting a new trans-ethnic people also got lost over the centuries. This loss somehow correlated with the way the functions of the special clergy had taken over defining and running the church.

THE REFORMATION THAT HAS YET TO HAPPEN

Of the five practices we are studying, this fourth one is the first that has not yet had its reformation. It is the first whose adequate concrete form has still to be retrieved. This specimen should make us aware that the New Testament contains resources for critique and renewal that have not yet been tapped. It should serve to warn us against the notion that there is one specific right model of reformation that, although it keeps getting lost, is always the same when it is found again.

Historically, in fact, there has been a striking degree of similarity in the renewal experiences represented by the Anabaptists of the sixteenth century, the Friends and Baptists of the seventeenth, the Wesleys of the eighteenth, or the Churches of Christ of the nineteenth. Still, though the notion of "restoring a biblical pattern" has an abiding appeal, it is too simple.

There is no one finished pattern of which particular free churches have the franchise. As the Puritan preacher John Robinson said, seeing off a shipload of his "pilgrim" brothers and sisters from Plymouth, England, for Massachusetts, "The Lord hath yet more light and truth to break forth from His holy Word." The Pauline vision of every-member empowerment is one fragment of the gospel vision that has yet to find its reformation, and it might be, by the nature of the case, that if it did happen it could not sweep across the map as some other reformations have.

What is sweeping across the map in our century is the debate about women in ministry. Assuming that there is one role called "ministry," whether sacerdotal or episcopal in focus, some denominations agree that women can carry that role, and others, both some of the very catholic and some of the very Protestant, deny it.

The mistake that dominates this debate, the reader will recognize, from the perspective of the Pauline vision, is not in the answers but in the question. There is not (i.e., there should not be) one "ministerial" role, of which then we could argue about whether it is gender specific. There are as many ministerial roles as there are members of the body of Christ, and that means that more than half of them belong to women. The roles *least justified* by the witness of the New Testament—quite regardless of the gender debate—are those of priest and of (supercongregational) bishop,[68] precisely the ones that some men have traditionally held alone and want to keep for themselves. To let a few women into an office that men have for generations wrongly restricted and that did not even exist in the apostolic churches may be a good kind of "affirmative action," but it is hardly the most profound vision of renewal. To debate about feminine access to the patriarchally defined ministry is like trying to say that Golda Meir, Margaret Thatcher, or Indira Gandhi transformed the nature of power politics.

The transformation that Paul's vision calls for would not be to let a few more especially gifted women share with a few men the rare roles of domination; it would be to reorient the notion of ministry so that there would be no one ungifted, no one not called, no one not empowered, and no one dominated. Only that would live up to Paul's call to "lead a life worthy of our calling."

5

The Rule of Paul

In the fourteenth chapter of his letter to the Christians at Corinth, the Apostle Paul instructs his readers about how to hold a meeting in the power of the Spirit. The wider context of this guidance is his vision of the unity of the body, which had been guiding his counsel all through the epistle. Its narrower context is his description of the Spirit-driven unity of the body, which had been his theme since Chapter 12. In this chapter his focus is narrower. Concretely, now the question is: How should a meeting of the church proceed? (The text is long and complex: I do not reproduce it here, but the reader should look it up).

Paul tells his readers that everyone who has something to say, something given by the Holy Spirit to him or her to say, can have the floor. The others who were speaking before are instructed to yield the floor to him or her.

Within this freedom for all to speak, a relative priority should be given to the mode of speech called "prophecy," because it speaks "to improve, to encourage, and to console." It is noteworthy that there is no reference to a single moderator, "minister," or "priest" governing the process, as things tend to proceed in most Christian groups in our time. Paul wishes that everyone might prophesy, perhaps echoing Moses' words to the same effect from Numbers 11:29, to which I already alluded on page 56 when the theme was how individuals are endowed by God with distinctive gifts. The other members of the church are instructed to "weigh" what the prophet has said. The only further instructions given are that the meeting is to be orderly and that anyone wishing to speak in an unknown tongue should only do so if a translation can be provided.

Readers of our generation find a special problem with two

verses toward the end of the chapter: "Women should be silent in the churches. For they are not permitted to speak" (vv. 34,35). These words cannot mean (for Paul) what they have usually been taken to say, namely that women should *literally* have no role in the church (as social body) or in the meeting. Paul had just written in Chapter 11 of the same epistle about women who should stand up to pray and prophesy. In Chapter 12 he had just spelled out at length how every member of the community—certainly not only the men—has a gift, and many of the gifts he named called for participating orally in meetings. In Chapter 16 he writes of Prisca leading the church in her home. What then does he mean here?[69] He is probably referring to chattering in the back rows, in which a woman, not very literate or well-informed, would ask her neighbor about what was being said. Paul writes (v. 35) that that kind of question can be taken care of at home, rather than taking over the meeting agenda with questions of clarification. Likewise a man not understanding something could ask his wife. But this does not modify in any way the woman's authority to speak in the meeting in her turn, and to be heard.

THE SAME EXPERIENCE IN ACTS

The same assumptions about the nature of a meeting were operative behind the narrative of Acts 15. A basic problem of missionary strategy was brought to the leadership of the church in Jerusalem. It was represented by missionaries who had been sent out by the church in Antioch, namely Paul and Barnabas. The question at stake then—which is not our present concern, but was our theme in Chapter 3—was the relations of Jews and Gentiles in the new churches. The procedure in the Jerusalem meeting was simple. Paul, Barnabas, and others from Antioch reported on their "field experience," namely about the way Gentiles had been joining their movement. Some Jerusalem believers objected that the proper rules for the induction of Gentiles into Judaism had not been followed. The senior apostle

Peter reminded the community of their earlier experiences related to the same issue in which he had led them, notably the Cornelius story (Acts 10).

According to Acts 15:12, this silenced the assembly. Paul and Barnabas then extended their account. When no one else had more to say, James, the senior elder of the congregation, proposed a mediating conclusion, of which he could say that it had "seemed good to the Holy Spirit and to us" (v. 28). The substance of the agreement was to authorize going ahead with Paul's vision of the unity of Jew and Gentile, which we discussed in Chapter 3 in connection with baptism.

Here in the Jerusalem meeting the concrete issue obliging them to make a decision was the application of the rules for table fellowship. Could Jews and Gentiles eat together in light of the Jewish rules about diet? The conclusion reached in the Jerusalem event largely overlaps with the guidance about dietary patterns in 1 Corinthians 8 and 10.

THE RULE OF PAUL IN
THE EARLY CHRISTIAN CENTURIES

When the churches that had been scattered around the Mediterranean world became aware both of their unity and of their differences, they recognized that it would be appropriate to extend beyond the local congregation that same pattern of decision making through open conversation. They called such meetings "synods" or "councils." The first such meetings were occasional, provoked by specific concerns about "heresy" or to try to resolve differences such as the one concerning a common date for Easter. With time, they came to be convened more regularly in the regions where Christians were sufficiently numerous. The larger and more regular these "councils" became, the more formal they had to be and the less they reflected spontaneity and the openness of the Jerusalem event.

In Cappadocia for example, synods were being held annually

by around the year 250. Beginning in the fourth century, major Councils were convened on an empirewide basis, called "ecumenical" (somewhat inaccurately because churches from outside the empire were not represented): Nicea (325), Constantinople (381), Ephesus (431), Chalcedon (451), Constantinople (553), and a handful more. Others continued to be convened, either regularly or occasionally, on national and regional levels.

When in the high Middle Ages more and more people became concerned about what they considered to be abuses in the life of the churches, the memory of that original apostolic council in Jerusalem and of the authority later ascribed by Christendom to the "ecumenical" councils came to mind. It came to be suggested that if a new "council" could be convened, truly representative of all Christendom, then God would again speak—despite the moral unworthiness of all the bishops and delegates severally—by creating in the power of the Spirit an authentic new unity of conviction, to renew the churches. In this unrealistic hope they telescoped the images of Jerusalem and of Nicea. They combined the image of a Spirit-moved deliberation and that of an empirewide political event. Historians call the advocates of this vision "conciliarists."

FIRST CORINTHIANS 14
AND THE PROTESTANT REFORMATION

The conciliarist hope, although it already had been frequently disappointed, was still alive when the Protestant movement began. Martin Luther, for instance, was quite confident that a true council, if one could be convened, would ratify his teaching. Yet that was a political impossibility. Neither the Holy Roman Empire nor the Vatican would convene such an event. In the absence of an ecumenical council, there was no available churchwide instrument to evaluate the theological legitimacy of the changes for which the reformation theologians were calling.

Ultimately it was decided that local governments could authorize those changes, but they hesitated at first to move ahead without someone to authorize them to do so. The solution that was found, especially in the upper Rhine Valley, was the "disputation." Local authorities borrowed this form of meeting from the university where it was the standard procedure for teaching and especially for authorizing a person's promotion to the office of *Magister* or *Doctor.*

In November 1522 Huldrych Zwingli, a priest already known as a popular preacher and patriot, began to work for the city fathers of Zurich instead of for the nearest Bishop. This changed assignment marked the beginning of what later history called the Protestant Reformation. Zwingli's pro-Roman critics objected to the city's employing a "heretic." In response, the city council fathers drew on the tradition I have been describing and convened a "disputation" for January 29, 1523. The university format of an open debate—with theses stated to be defended, a moderator, and a secretary—was joined to the idealism about Acts 15 and the instructions of 1 Corinthians 14.

Zwingli's critics failed to convince the councilmen that Zwingli was wrong (partly because the main critic, John Faber, representing the Bishop of Constance, denied the Zurich city government's right to do theology). Thus Zwingli's path was cleared for reform. The Council ruled that he could go on teaching "the pure Word of God." In the face of Faber's objections, Zwingli based his case on 1 Corinthians 14 and concluded that the local church has authority to act in such matters. Nine months later, specific issues of implementation, concerning the place of images in the churches and the fate of the Mass, were ready for action. Another disputation, under the same rules, was called for October 26, 1523.

Zwingli himself, however, did not trust this vision fully. Once he had the city fathers on his side, he equated them with the elders of the Jerusalem church. That meant that he thought they no longer needed to continue consulting with the community at large. From then on, the Reformation would be carried out by "Milords" of the Council—what we call "the state"—though for him there was no distinction between church and state. Yet Zwingli still acknowledged that what he called "the Rule of Paul," namely the freedom of all to speak according to this same passage, ought ideally to be respected more broadly. He-wrote in April 1525:

> In Zurich we do not yet practice the counsel of the congregation, but everyone has the right to go to the priest who teaches publicly,[70] and to address him where he believes that he has taught deceptively. . . . Now where such free intervention before the congregation would be fitting, let no-one doubt that the spirit of peace and concord would bring us into unity of belief and understanding.

At about the same time, Martin Luther was writing his tract, "That a Christian Assembly or Congregation has the Right and Power to Judge All Teaching and to Call, Appoint, and Discuss Teachers, Established and Proven by Scripture."[71] Amidst a flurry of prooftexts warning against false teachers and others describing the consent of local churches in the naming of their ministers, Luther also appealed (p. 310) to 1 Corinthians 14 as the warrant for a congregation's taking its order into its own hands.

Sometime around 1533 some Swiss Brethren[72] wrote a tract, which was preserved for us by their archenemy Heinrich Bullinger. This "Answer of Some who are Called Anabaptists, Why They do not Attend the Churches"[73] gives six reasons for not attending the state church preaching services. "The first reason is that they [i.e., the Reformed state church preachers] do not observe the Christian order as taught in the gospel or the word of God in 1 Cor. 14, namely, that a listener is bound by Christian love (if something to edification is given or revealed to him) that he should and may speak of it also in the congregation. . . ."

GOD'S WILL IS KNOWN
BY THE SPIRIT WORKING IN THE MEETING

In sum: All across the beginning Protestant movement, we can observe the same theologically motivated conviction about the process whereby God's will is made known. Independently in all the early Protestant movements, this conviction was understood to be prefigured in and mandated specifically by 1 Corinthians 14. Consensus arises uncoerced out of open conversation. There is no voting in which a majority overruns a minority and no decision of a leader by virtue of his office. The only structure this process needs is the moderating that keeps it orderly and the recording of the conclusions reached.

All of this was well on the way long before the Reformation moved to Great Britain; there the same ideas were bound to be encountered again. From the Netherlands a few British "Baptists" had received these "radically reformed" ideas, but many more within England came to the same convictions along their own paths. The indigenous "Puritan" movement was progressively radicalized beyond Presbyterianism to Congregationalism, beyond congregationalism to "independentism" and Baptism, and beyond that to the Seekers, Levellers, the Friends, and the Ranters.[74] All of that movement made much of the demand that the gospel be freely preached and freely heard. Not only for the sake of the church but also for the sake of the secular society— Puritans demanded freedom of assembly, of preaching, and of the press—all across the spectrum from John Milton to George Fox, as extensions of the franchise of 1 Corinthians 14.

Historian Baron A.D. Lindsay is credited with giving wide currency to the idea that Anglo-Saxon democracy (different in important ways from the enlightenment democracy of Latin Europe) is an extension of the Puritan vision of the hearers freely gathered under the preaching of the Word and free to talk back to the expositor, as he is their servant, not a mouthpiece of the king, the bishop, or the university.

Because the Seekers and the Levellers did not survive and

because the Baptists retained the pastor-centered forms of earlier Puritanism, it was left to the Friends to work through most
thoroughly and self-consciously the understanding of how the
Spirit of Christ is present in all members to shape and guide the
church. Quaker silence in meeting is not, as some have thought
more recently, a form of elite mysticism or a "silent worship." It
is a time of expectant waiting until someone—and the point is
that it can and will be anyone—is moved to utterance. There is
in this respect no formal difference between a meeting for
worship and one for deliberation. Until the consensus becomes
clear, as it became in Jerusalem through the silence of all other
voices, no decision has been reached. There is special concern
not to overrule the unconvinced by majority vote or parliamen-
tary closure and not to miss the voices of the absent. Until
everyone with something to say has had the floor and until
those who care have talked themselves out, the Spirit's will is
not clearly known.

Because Quakers can do this in meetings for worship and in
deliberation, they can do it as well in mission. A meeting for
worship "after the manner of Friends" and a meeting for business have the same shape and operate under the same rules. The
administrators of a relief agency such as the Friends Service
Committee or of a Quaker college use the same format of
unscripted openness, listening to the Spirit speaking through
each other, and consensus. It is also the Friends who have found
special ways to bring together the representatives of warring
parties—in Northern Ireland or the Middle East, for instance,
especially in United Nations circles—to foster the potential for
dialogue among individuals even when their institutional loyalties are in conflict.[75]

George Fox had said that as he roamed around Britain he was
"speaking to that of God in every person." Later Friends apply
that image, positing in every person whom one addresses some
divinely imparted potential to hear, not only to the baptized
nominal Christians of England three centuries ago, but to
anyone they meet. That is not a generalized humanism but a

careful rendering of the passage in John that affirms that what became human in Jesus was already present throughout creation enlightening everyone (John 1:9).

Obviously, when the trust that truth will be found in open conversation is extended beyond the messianic community, there are fewer common landmarks. The common language will be more "secular." The moral consensus that such dialogue can apply will be thinner. Yet the reason for engaging that dialogue is no less the conviction that, in the age of Jesus the Messiah, the healing resources of his ministry can by the nature of things reach farther than the knowledge of his name and that among these healing resources is the commitment to hear not only the neighbor but even the adversary.

The commitment to hear even the adversary projects two very modern implications. One is what Gandhi meant by characterizing his life as "experimenting with truth." The reason one renounces violence in social conflict, said Gandhi, is not (not only, not merely) that bloodshed is morally forbidden; it is that the adversary is part of my truth-finding process. I need to act nonviolently in order to get the adversary to hear me, but I need as well to hear the adversary.

A second is the new awareness in our generation of the special commitment and special instruments that are indispensable if the voice of the underdog is to be heard. Liberation theologians today speak of "the epistemological privilege of the oppressed." There is no blunter instrument to guarantee such a hearing for hitherto inadequately spoken-for causes than to remember Paul's simple rule that everyone must be given the floor.

THE SPECTER OF ANARCHY

But can we afford to let local meetings in every place claim the same freedom for all to speak and for conclusions to be validated by consensus? Will the result not be chaotic diversity? That has always been the standard fear of the threatened paternalists. A small part, and a reasonable part of the answer is to

say that such decentralization, founded in the belief that the
Spirit speaks to and through everyone, will enable wholesome
and realistic flexibility in adapting to local occasions and needs.
The stronger, more theological, part of the answer is, however,
that because Jesus Christ is always and everywhere the same,
any procedure that yields sovereignty to the direction of his
spirit will have ultimately to create unity. What does not create
authentic unity is the centralized power tactics of the Caesars,
the Inquisitors, or any other patriarchs or paternalists. A monarchical decree is quicker than careful listening, but is usually
wrong. A quick majority vote may reach a decision more rapidly
but without resolving the problem or convincing the over-
powered minority, so that the conflict remains. Quaker consensus modes of decision, as I said, can administer a relief agency or
a college just as efficiently as can the "corporate models" to
which Presbyterians and United Methodists are accustomed.
United Methodists know that annual conference decisions or
congregational ones reached by a bare majority create new
problems for the future.

   This "apostolic practice" is perhaps simpler than the others as
far as what the Bible says is concerned, so that our describing it
has taken fewer pages. Because God the Spirit speaks in the
meeting, conversation is the setting for truth-finding. That is
true in the local assembly and in wider assemblies, in the faith
community and in wider groups.

6

Conclusion

Now we have walked through our survey of five sample "practices."[76] This prepares us to ask some wider questions. Each of these practices can stand alone, with its own worth, its own objectives, its own way of making sense. I suggested at the outset that they would demonstrate parallel traits. Now it will be appropriate to look back across the series and see whether that is the case. What generalizations might we draw from the five specimens?

THE NOTION OF "SACRAMENT": HUMAN ACTION IN WHICH GOD ACTS

These last two specimens of prescribed social process, "the rule of Paul" (decision by means of conversation) and the varieties of roles, like the first practice we studied ("binding and loosing"), do *not* fall within what ordinarily is called "worship," even less "liturgy." Yet why should they not be so designated? Each is a practice, which can be described formally and which is carried out when believers gather for reasons evidently derived from their faith. Each is a way God acts. Each is capable of being illuminated by doctrinal elaboration. Each of the practices is described as involving both divine and human action, and as mandatory. For each, it makes a difference whether it is done rightly or wrongly. I suggest that we should perhaps conclude that the odd selectivity whereby most of the churches lifted up two "sacraments"[77] and forgot the rest is without theological warrant.

All five of the practices we have been reviewing can be spoken

71

of in social process terms. They can be translated into non-religious terms. The multiplicity of gifts is a model for the empowerment of the humble and the end of hierarchy in social process. Dialogue under the Holy Spirit is the ground floor of the notion of democracy. Admonition to bind or loose at the point of offense is the foundation for conflict resolution and consciousness-raising. Baptism enacts interethnic social acceptance, and breaking bread celebrates economic solidarity.

Our concern here is neither to discuss the medieval changes that led to the evolution of the "magical" or "superstitious" notion of "sacrament" nor to analyze with the historian's care the extent to which some experiences of reformation or renewal over the centuries were able to retrieve this or that strand of the original vision. Our concern here is rather to renew the search for what might today be a valid, theologically appropriate vision of "sacraments" in whatever sense of the term we find most meaningful and responsible.

Baptists and other free churches have tended to abandon the word *sacrament* to the opposition, letting it retain the magical or mechanical and priest-centered overtones that had discredited the mainline usage. Baptists have used instead the word *ordinance.*

There may be situations of controversial renewal or ecumenical debate where that recourse, letting the adversaries write the dictionary and abandoning words that have been "spoiled," is inescapable; but there should be other times, in settings where we can choose our language carefully and define our own terms, when we could reverse the strategy and claim the old language for the original proper meanings. I plan to do the same thing, as the reader will see, with the contested old word *evangelical.*

In that basic "lay" sense of a human action in which God is active, all of these five practices—fraternal admonition, the open meeting, and the diversification of gifts, no less than the other practices of baptism and Eucharist—are worship, are ministry, are doxology (praise), are celebratory, and are mandatory. They are actions of God, in and with, through and under what men and women do. Where they are happening, the people of God is real in the world.

Although atypical and nontraditional, these activities are not esoteric or difficult to understand. They are publicly accessible behaviors, which the neighbors cannot merely notice but in fact share in, understand, and imitate. Whether this means they should be called ordinances, as Baptists and Brethren prefer, or sacraments, as the "high" traditions do (but with a "low" meaning), I don't mind letting the reader decide.

There is another set of terms, of themes, to which we need also to relate our "five practices." Terms such as *spiritual discipline* have recently become familiar (or become familiar again). Modes of prayer, meditation, counseling, devotional practices, and spiritual direction, which were once automatically taken for granted in church-dominated cultures, today come to be taken up again by some as voluntary disciplines. These activities are like the ones we have been studying here, in that they make the Christian life a matter of direct attention and intention. Such disciplines certainly will support and be supported by the "five practices"; they differ in their interpersonal, even institutional concreteness.

THE SHAPE OF "POLITICAL" FAITHFULNESS

Along the way I paused occasionally to draw attention to the way in which this particular New Testament vision differs from the dominant mental patterns of recent Western social-ethical thought. Now it is time to tie together the description of this distinctiveness in a synthesis.

All of the strands I shall mention here have run through the earlier description of the five faith practices, although there was not time to seek to accentuate each of them in every setting.

In an ideal compendium one might attempt to chart an encyclopedic grid, following each of these practices (and perhaps one or two more[78])through the history from ancient Israel, through the Judaism of the dispersion, to Jesus, and from there through the later history, especially the history of free church renewal, to the present. In the absence of that full chart, I trust that the global impression is firm enough in the reader's mind to permit generalizing. Especially I shall be interested in any possible general lessons concerning the question with which our study began, namely how the gospel impinges on the rest of our world.

A. **Which is the "real world"?** Whereas contemporary dominant mental habits assume that there is "out there" an objective or agreed account of reality and that faith perspectives must come to terms with that wider picture by fitting into it, as a subset of the generally unbelieving worldview. I propose rather that we recognize that we are called to a believing vision of global history, suspicious of any scheme of analysis or management that would claim by itself to see the world whole apart from faith or apart from avowing its own bias. The modern world is a subset of the world vision of the gospel, not the other way around. That means we can afford to begin with the gospel notions themselves and then work out from there, as our study has done, rather than beginning with the "real world" out there (someone else's definition of "the nature of things") and then trying to place the call of God within it.

B. **Respect the world's unbelief.** Christian discipleship is derived from faith in Christ; it is therefore not something we could transpose without "mediation" or "translation" to the social structures not derived from that faith. That is the *partial* truth of Luther's saying that "you cannot rule the world by the gospel." Luther thought this meant that we must look for another kind of "political" guidance, other than the gospel, with which to rule the world. The simpler view would be that we can serve the world but are not called to rule it.

C. **Real common agenda.** There is however a kind of mediation, a "bridging-over," which our five "practices" illustrate, from the faith community to the other social structures. This kind of "mediation" is not a mental or verbal operation of translation or conceptual bridging, but rather the concrete historical presence, among their neighbors, of believers who for Jesus' sake do ordinary social things differently. They fraternize trans-ethnically; they share their bread; they forgive one another. These activities are visible; they are not opaque rituals. They lend themselves to being observed, imitated, and extrapolated.

D. **No dichotomy of substance.** This mediation or "kingdom presence" rejects, as classical social ethics affirmed, that there should be a firm dualism separating Christ from culture or law from gospel or creation from redemption. According to those dichotomies, ethics—or social ethics—can and should be less authentically derived from the gospel than should Christian thought and witness in any other realm of discourse. The major Christian traditions (Roman Catholic, Lutheran, and Calvinist) make this split in different ways.

E. **Not to rule but to serve.** The image guiding the Christian presence in the world is not one of sovereignty, whereby we should increasingly bring it about that the world should be ruled by believers (or by their ideas), but of servanthood. We have been trained to give priority to lordship models of social process, whereby the Lord makes laws and the bureaucrat implements them.

F. **Gospel.** All of the "five practices" and all of these aspects they have in common, can be called "good news." This is the original meaning of the noun *gospel* and of the adjective *evangelical.* I call it "evangelical" first because it communicates "news." It says something that people will not know if they are not told. This news must secondly be accredited as "good"; it comes across to those who hear it as helpful, saving, and healing. News is by definition always public; it is proclaimed in the open. It cannot be esoteric or private and be news. Yet the way for it to be "good news" is not to try to please some marketplace or live up to someone else's prior picture of what is creditable. The message does not become good news by abstracting or distilling something out of the particular Jewishness or first-centuriness of the original story of Jesus and his disciples.

As noted in Chapter 3, all of these practices are derived from the redemptive work of Christ, not from some other level of the knowledge of God in unfallen creation or timeless reason. This makes them no less public. It makes them more realistic about sin and more hopeful about reconciliation than are those approaches that trust the nature/reason complex to derive the knowledge of what should be from what is.

G. As a body. In contrast to the standard approaches, these practices do not make the individual the pivot of change. The individual is neither forgotten nor relativized; what could be more tailored-to-measure than the notion of a unique charisma? Nothing honors the underdog more than the authorization to take the floor. Yet no trust is placed in the individual's changed "insights" or "insides" to change the world. The fulcrum for change and the forum for discernment is the moral independence of the believing community as a body.

H. And the state? For reasons I have not sought to explain, my entire exposition has given less attention to the issues of state coercion and war than to other themes, and less than the Gospel account does.[79] We could have gone through the evidence concerning Jesus' being attracted by and yet rejecting the Zealot conception of Messiah's calling. We would have seen the importance of his (and therefore of our) rejection of lordship models of doing the truth. His choice of servanthood was in fact part of the meaning of all five of the practices we have reviewed. A Zealot liberator (a Jewish Che Guevara) would have sent the rich away empty and might have fed the crowd in the desert and would have freed the prisoners, but he would hardly have ordained Hellenists to make sure the widows got fed. He would have upset the social fruit basket but would not have proclaimed the charismatic authority of every member of the body. He might have baptized people fearful of the coming judgment, demanding works worthy of repentance, but he would hardly have made Jew and Gentile, male and female equal in dignity. Under "new humanity" we learn to reject violence because nationalism is always ethnic. Nonviolence belongs under reconciliation (binding and loosing) because war is an alternative to forgiveness and under sharing because war is practically always for economics. Thus all of the five practices spell out in different ways the fundamental decision of Jesus to accept the conditions of suffering servanthood as the shape of his messiahship.

I. **Command.** The authority for these practices is revealed; it is part of the intervention into history which we call incarnation or redemption. Jesus told people to do them. He did so in God's name, assuring his disciples that God would empower their doing them. That transcendent mandate is why I have suggested that the label *sacrament* could be appropriate (*if* we can purge it of distracting medieval meanings). As I have said before, it makes a difference whether they are done rightly or wrongly.

J. **Paradigm.** Yet as we saw, they are not "ritual" or "religious" in any otherworldly sense (any more than the humanity of Jesus was). What they are doing can be spoken of in social process terms, which can easily be transposed into non-religious equivalents that a sociologist could watch. People who do not share the faith or join the community can learn from them. "Binding and loosing" can provide models for conflict resolution, alternatives to litigation, and alternative perspectives on "corrections." Sharing bread is a model not only for soup kitchens and hospitality houses, but also for Social Security and negative income tax. "Every member has a gift" is an immediate alternative to vertical "business" models of management. Open dialogue correlates with why the Japanese make better cars than Detroit. Dialogue under the Holy Spirit is the ground floor of the notion of democracy. And so on. . . .

For us to approach social ethics in this light will not lead us to differ at every point from what others have been saying on other grounds as to the immediate dictates for our contemporary caring. What will differ from other approaches is its shape as a whole; namely, the conception that the Christian social ethical witness must be defined not by its independence from the witness of the faith community[80] but by its derivation therefrom.

The believing body is the image that the new world—which in the light of the ascension and Pentecost is on the way—casts ahead of itself. The believing body of Christ is the world on the way to its renewal; the church is the part of the world that confesses the renewal to which all the world is called. The believing body is the instrument of that renewal of the world, to the (very modest) extent to which its message is faithful. It may be "instrument" as proclaimer, or as pilot project, or as pedestal.

For the people of God to be over against the world at those points where "the world" is defined by its rebellion against God and for us to be in, with, and for the world, as anticipation of the shape of redemption, are not alternative strategies. We are not free to choose between them, depending on whether our tastes are more "catholic" or more "baptist,"[81] or depending on whether we think the times are friendly just now or not. Each dimension of our stance is the prerequisite for the validity of the other. A church that is not "against the world" in fundamental ways has nothing worth saying to and for the world.[82] Conversion and separation are not the way to become otherworldly; they are the only way to be present, relevantly and redemptively, in the midst of things.

Long ago, the French Reformed lay theologian Jacques Ellul wrote a book titled *The Presence of the Kingdom,* arguing that, for the witnessing community, the very fact that we stand in the midst of the world is more basic for what God wants to see happen than are the particular projects Christians might undertake. A half-generation later, Ellul had to write *False Presence of the Kingdom*, objecting to the use that had been made of his slogan to justify too simply claiming this or that set of institutions or events as God's cause. It was not that Ellul changed his mind; it was rather that loving the world and refusing conformity to it, being present in its midst and being a foreign body, are not opposite ends of a scale, components which one is free to choose between or to mix as one pleases, but two sides of a coin, both always necessarily present.

IS THIS A PATTERN?

Looking back at the ground we have covered together, one more question arises about the shape of my presentation. The five expositions have been formally parallel. Standing on the shoulders of some Hebrew precedents (though without pursuing them at depth), we have seen each of the five "practices" represented in rather simple form in the New Testament. We have seen that each theme has fallen and risen again, been forgotten and surfaced again, over the centuries. Of each we have seen that it can reach beyond the church into the world, helping give shape to our general human hope.

Should I then take one step farther and claim that my general approach is "true" *because* the substance is there and has this shape, in such a way that each major subject can unfold along similar lines? Have we happened onto a deep logic in the nature of things?

I would not claim so much. There may very well be themes that would not in the same way lend themselves to exposition along this outline. There might be some subjects where what has to be said about the church could not be extrapolated for the world in the same way. There may be components of discipleship, important for both church and world, which are not covered by these five practices and where the neat symmetry of a New Testament "sacrament" might not apply. There might be themes for which the testimony of the New Testament does not in the same sense "fulfill" that of the Old.

Yet neither do I want to be too modest. It should not be surprising if there were such a deep structure that, once discerned in the five places where we have touched it, would then illuminate more broadly the shape of all of God's saving purposes. For other theological systems the claimed deep structure is an intellectual construct, such as the duality of nature and grace, or of law and gospel, or vestiges of the Trinity. Why should it not be the case that God's purpose for the world would pursue an organic logic through history and across the agenda of the pilgrim people's social existence with such a reliable rhythm as we have here observed?

ENDNOTES

1. We shall return to the classical statement of this notion in the Declaration of Independence of the United States: "We hold these truths to be self-evident."
2. We shall return to this theme in Chapter 4.
3. Each of the chapters here is distilled from a much wider body of biblical, historical, and social-scientific wisdom, very little of it original to me. References in the other notes will point to some further resources for study.
4. Henceforth I shall be using the term *church*, as the Bible does, to name this "community held together by commitment to important values." Yet we need to be warned against some of the overtones which the term has taken on over the years. The accent is not on a clerical or bureaucratic management structure or on a denomination. Of course it is not on a building. It is on people who relate to one another on the grounds of their shared faith.
5. The Greek word *polis*, from which as I indicated *political* is derived, is often translated "city." It does not mean just the streets and houses, the space on the map, or just the people; it means the orderly way in which they live together and make decisions, the way they structure their common life.
6. In Chapter 4 I shall note especially that on the matter that concerns us, the Apostle Paul did not speak for all of the churches. Something of the same kind should be said about every reading of the Bible. None of the New Testament—not even Acts, which reads most like a history book—claims to be simply describing the early church as it was.
7. The Greek term that is often translated "brothers" here is masculine, but is not gender-exclusive. The phrase "against you," which appears in some translations, does not belong in the text, as we shall see later.
8. My own translation, because NRSV and RSV both need correcting.
9. These three metaphorical prepositions were standard usage in the Protestant doctrine of the sacraments in the sixteenth century.
10. I studied this material in June 1980 with Baptists in Australia, in addition to the Methodist and Lutheran groups named in the Preface.
11. Cf. also the duty to be reconciled in Matt. 5:24.
12. Cf. Note 9 above.

13. Not widely remembered by nonhistorians, Martin Bucer was the senior reformer of the city of Strasbourg from 1522 to 1543. Contemporary and peer of Luther and Huldrych Zwingli, he was more moderate than they and more concerned about personal pastoral care. He was the predecessor and mentor of John Calvin, thereby father of the "Reformed" strand of the Protestant movement, which went on via Geneva to Scotland, the Netherlands, and England.

14. Distant ancestors of the Mennonite, Hutterian, Amish, and Baptist visions of Reformation.

15. The most prominent Reformer of Zurich from 1519 to 1531.

16. Müntzer was a visionary reformer who first came to a visible leadership role in the early 1520s within the Lutheran movement, which he soon rejected for its insufficient radicality; ultimately Müntzer allied himself with the peasants' rebellion of 1524-1525.

17. Leland Harder, ed., *The Sources of Swiss Anabaptism* (Scottdale: Herald Press, 1985), pp. 284ff. Although the phenomena then called "anabaptist" by its critics were very diverse, not really one movement, this group at Zurich in 1524 projected the stance which ultimately came to characterize the "Swiss Brethren, "Hutterian," and "Mennonite" movements.

18. H. Wayne Pipkin and J. Yoder, eds., *Balthasar Hubmaier: Theologian of Anabaptism* (Scottdale: Herald Press, 1989), pp. 372ff.

19. John Wesley, "The Cure of Evil-Speaking" in *The Works of John Wesley*, Vol. 2, *Sermons II*, Edited by Albert C. Outler, (Nashville, TN: Abingdon Press, 1985), pp. 251-62. According to Outler, the roots of this sermon were in a pact with fellow Methodists to avoid speaking ill of persons behind their backs, and to discuss any problems or charges face to face. Wesley preached on the subject a number of times in 1752, then periodically in 1753, 1758, 1786, and 1787.

20. Alexander Campbell was the best known of the founders of the renewal movement in the middle of the nineteenth century in the middle of America, variously known as "restoration," "Churches of Christ," or "Disciples." One of his convictions was that the "New Testament pattern" for the life of the church was clearly accessible to all believers in the apostolic texts.

21. The technical term *adiaphoron,* something which makes no difference, was used by Lutherans for the realm of church order.

22. The field of publication, research, and training is enormous. Conflict resolution has its own schools and professional organizations. For an introduction, see Roger Fisher and William Ury, *Getting to Yes: Negotiating Agreement Without Giving In* (New York: Penguin, 1983) or Christopher W. Moore, *The Mediation Process* (San Francisco: Jossey-Bass, 1987).

23. Howard Zehr, *Mediating the Victim-Offender Conflict* (Akron, PA: Mennonite Central Committee).

24. Just for emphasis, I remind the reader that my concern for understanding

the New Testament is not a picky fundamentalist one; my intention is honestly to help the scriptures function as they were intended to—as our guide in faith and practice.

25. The Jubilee provisions of Leviticus 25 and Deuteronomy 15 are interpreted in my *Politics of Jesus* (Grand Rapids: Eerdmans, 1972), pp. 64ff. We shall return to this theme toward the end of the chapter.

26. *Hellenist* does not mean "Greek," as the King James had it, but Greek-speaking Jews, namely Jews who had previously lived outside of Palestine, where Greek was the common language.

27. In Chapter 5 we shall return to study Acts 15 as a specimen of how the Holy Spirit guides discernment in dialogue. There we shall see that event as exemplifying how the apostolic community, led by the Spirit of God, made an important strategic decision. Here we are observing why the decision was important, which underlines the centrality of table fellowship as mission.

28. Many scholars and pastoral thinkers have begun to make more of the "meal" dimension of the Eucharist. In lieu of an ambitious bibliography I limit myself to one very old source and one more recent one: Norman Fox, *Christ in the Daily Meal* (New York: Fords, Howard and Halbert, 1898) and Arthur Cochrane, *Eating and Drinking with Jesus* (Philadelphia: Westminster, 1974).

29. I already noted the inadequacy of the "Enlightenment" notion that everyone was "endowed by their creator with inalienable rights."

30. G. Wainwright, *Eucharist and Eschatology,* Oxford.

31. Cf. Philip Hallie, *Lest Innocent Blood Be Shed.*

32. In order to render the meaning most clearly, I am mixing phrases from the NEB and the NRSV.

33. The King James Version says, "If any man is in Christ *he* is a new *creature."* This has led to countless arguments about how the new creating that God does in the new birth relates to the rest of the world. There is no New Testament warrant for rendering the Greek word *ktisis* as designating an individual. The paraphrases by Phillips and Taylor make the same mistake worse. I have explained at length the reasons for the rightness of the NEB translation and the difference it makes in "The Apostle's Apology Revisited." Cf. Note 35.

34. Cf. my text "The Social Shape of the Gospel" in Wilbert R. Shenk (ed.), *Exploring Church Growth,* pp. 277-84, especially 280ff. Paul's missionary/pastoral method and his message were inseparable.

35. One of the marks of a valid induction, one way of insuring that the meaning we find in a text is not our own invention, is that we happen upon this kind of parallelism, where the same point is made in different settings with more than one set of words. My *The Politics of Jesus,* pp. 135-62 and 215-32 and my "The Apostle's Apology Revisited" in Wm. Klassen (ed.)

The New Way of Jesus (Scottdale: Herald, 1980), pp. 115-34 summarize the further argument behind this interpretation.

36. Cf. the reference to "my mystery" in Note 34.

37. Scripture scholars are not sure that the apostle himself wrote the letter to the Ephesians; if he did not, this testimony of his followers to the meaning of the message arising from his ministry would be no weaker. Some scripture scholars warn against assuming too much agreement between Paul's own writings and the narrative of Acts, but at this point Acts does describe Paul's unique ministry largely in terms of the Jew/Gentile bridge.

38. Acts 17:18; it would seem that superficial Athenian listeners thought that *anastasis* (resurrection) was the name of a second "foreign deity" in addition to Jesus.

39. The "soldiers" who came to hear John were part of the hated Roman occupation, although they might have been Jews or other Semites under Herod's command.

40. We have already met Zwingli (Note 13) in connection with Anabaptist origins. The radical Zwinglians who became Anabaptists initially took over from him something of this cognitive flattening of the meaning of symbols, but they took baptism more seriously than that. They were so concerned with restoring the (adult) voluntariness, which baptism had had in the beginning, that they were willing to be persecuted to the death for being baptized upon the confession of their faith.

41. We must, however, acknowledge a difference. Whereas the breaking of bread in a communion ceremony still resembles *somewhat* a real meal, the link between baptism as a ritual washing and the overcoming of ethnicity is not as evident.

42. There will be room for debate about infant baptism in the light of this meaning. The argument against infant baptism, which would follow from this understanding of baptism, would not be the same as for the cognitive "Baptist" argument cited above.

43. Allen O. Miller (ed.), *A Christian Declaration on Human Rights* (Grand Rapids: Eerdmans, 1977) provides the best statement of an interpretation of "human rights" in the Reformed tradition, founded in the sovereignty and Word of God rather than in an Enlightenment vision of the intrinsic dignity of the individual.

44. The appeal to creation is of course classically used in favor of ethnic segregation rather than equality.

45. These hard-to-define slogans were at the heart of the program of the 1963 Assembly of the Division of World Mission and Evangelism of the World Council of Churches, meeting at Mexico City.

46. If, for instance, you are trying to evangelize white racists in Mississippi in 1960, can you accept their racism by having segregated services in order

to reach them with your evangelistic message, counting on their Christian experience and education to overcome their racism later?

47. For two centuries the term *Great Commission* has been the code label for Matthew 28:20: "Make disciples of all nations, as you go, baptizing them, teaching them. . . . " This was understood as the most specific statement of the missionary imperative the church was called to obey. In the beginning of the modern missionary movement, there were debates about whether this command was still binding or whether perhaps the apostles had already done it. Often the first words, "Go ye, "were accentuated, although in the Greek that is said adverbially, as it is rendered above: "As you go. . . . "

48. An excellent selection from a much wider debate in the world of mission theology is provided by Wilbert R. Shenk (ed.), *The Challenge of Church Growth: A Symposium* (Elkhart, Indiana: 1973) and W. T. Shenk (ed.) *Exploring Church Growth* (Grand Rapids: Eerdmans, 1983), especially my "The Social Shape of the Gospel" in the latter text, pp. 277-84.

49. Donald McGavran, *The Bridges of God* (London: World Dominion Press, 1955); *Eye of the Storm* (World Books, 1972).

50. What is meant by "the powers" is capsuled in Chapter 8 of my *Politics of Jesus,* pp. 135ff.

51. Although what was in fact mostly at stake legally in the origins of religious liberty was the freedom to form voluntary associations, the form the public debate took in seventeenth century England was centered upon freedom of speech. Thus *preaching* and *assembly* rather than *baptism* were the fulcrum terms around which our English common-law culture's thought about religious liberty developed. The United States Bill of Rights says *free exercise,* a term that is vague but includes them all.

52. H. Richard Niebuhr qualified as "christomonism" a view which would not affirm that there are things we know about the will of God by way of the Father, or of the Spirit, which are different from and (for some cultural purposes) more important than following Jesus.

53. This distinction was made in the keynote sermon presented by Lutheran theologian Joseph Sittler at the 1961 New Delhi Assembly of the World Council of Churches. The 1961 theme was "Jesus Christ, the Light of the World." From some perspectives, the Jesus of history is too particular to be the light *of the world.* Whatever the value of that argument in "some perspectives," it seems to meet no need in the present study because the things Jesus says are in no way peculiar or esoteric; they can apply to anyone. Neither the Father nor the Spirit nor the Trinity as a whole says something else.

54. I have left these two words of jargon in the text to signal both that I respect my academic colleagues with their complex method questions and

that I do not take them *too* seriously. *Epistemological* means having to do with how we know, and *prolegomena* means what must come before something else. Some think that before doing what Jesus says, we need a theory about why to trust the report or why to do it.

55. The newer translations NEB and NRSV, by changing the word order, favor the mistaken understanding that the passage is about *individual* maturation and "stature." The reader would do well to reread carefully the entire passage, verses 1-14.

56. The entire passage, 12:3-31, is one literary unit, and in fact the much better known Chapter 13 is a commentary on it.

57. For Catholics this special function is celebrating the eucharist; for fundamentalists it is preaching. For others it may be leadership in social action or pastoral counseling. What the person does is less important for definition of the need for the role than the fact that the person is set apart. I have shown in my fuller treatment *The Fullness of Christ* that the role of religious specialist is deeply rooted anthropologically. It is a transcultural constant. When I use the term *priestly* or where the anthropologist uses the technical equivalent *sacerdotal*, we do not mean only the special role of offering sacrifices, but *any* function that monopolizes the link with God.

58. I am very much in favor of all of these modern experiences; nonetheless, they are feeble analogues, not equivalents to what Paul is talking about. His vision is richer and newer.

59. These are technical terms from European and Roman Catholic social thought, which seek to understand and guide group life with less respect for the individual's uniqueness. The reader who is unfamiliar with them should not worry because Paul's answer is better and includes what they say that is of value.

60. This is the Greek word we translate "church," but it also means "deliberative assembly" or even "parliament."

61. The reader may want to compare and contrast the several lists. A review of New Testament thought, including a chart of these lists, is provided in my booklet *The Fullness of Christ* (Elgin, IL: Brethren Press, 1987), pp. 9-14.

62. "Not many of you should become teachers" (James 3:1). The reason James gives is that language ("the tongue") is ungovernable. "Avoid wrangling over words" (1 Tim. 2:14).

63. In academic culture, anthropology means the historical and systematic study of human cultures. In theology it means the doctrine of human nature. Both senses are fitting here.

64. The other "office" that later became central, which also was absent in the New Testament, was the "bishop" exercising authority over a large number of local parishes without being subject to any of them. This is to say

nothing of archbishops, patriarchs, or popes, whose positions were not regularized for centuries.

65. This is the primary theme of Hebrews 7:1-10:19.

66. One of the easy errors we make in reading the Bible is to project medieval assumptions back into earlier times. There was some kind of a "bishop" in Rome before the end of the first century, but there was no "pope" (in the Roman Catholic sense) there for centuries. Nor was there uniformity among all the churches in any matters of doctrine or practice.

67. A standard misreading of history is the assumption that all the early Christians had our New Testament or that it speaks for all of them. In fact, many churches in the first century probably never heard of Paul. Others, which heard of him, never acknowledged his authority. Others may have affirmed his authority but without really understanding his message. Thus our concern to understand and implement the apostolic vision must not be misunderstood as positing that there was once a single universally implemented pattern, which we can simply describe, and which then at some later time was betrayed or rejected.

68. When (rarely) the word *episcopos* (literally "overseer"), which we translate "bishop," occurs in the New Testament, it describes a leadership role within the local congregation, not different from "shepherd." The notion of an officer over a large district ("diocese") is not in the New Testament.

69. Some scholars suggest that these two verses, which constitute an interruption in the flow of the text, were not in Paul's original text, but were added later. That may the case, but there is no ancient manuscript without them. Simply to set them aside seems to me to be a too-easy answer. Even if someone else wrote them later, they should mean something compatible with the rest of the epistle. The last words of the paragraph, "Did the Word of God originate with you?" seem in any case to reach back to the broad teaching of vv. 32f, rather than to the question of women speaking.

70. The "priest who teaches publicly" is of course himself. It did not occur to Zwingli to note that in the 1 Corinthians passage there was no reference to such a central single leader.

71. *Luther's Works*, Vol. 39, pp. 301ff.

72. This is the most appropriate name for the local variety of the "left wing of the [Swiss] Reformation," which were then called "anabaptist" by their persecutors.

73. Paul Peachey, ed., "Answer of some . . . ," *Mennonite Quarterly Review* 45 (1971), pp. 5-32.

74. From the considerable confusion of these several British movements between 1690 and 1760, there survived the movements we know as Presbyterian, Congregationalist, Baptist, and Quaker.

75. I have described the effectiveness of Quaker peacemaking activities in my

booklet *Nevertheless: The Varieties and Shortcomings of Religious Pacifism* (Herald Press, 1992), pp. 145ff.

76. I chose the term *practice* as the most neutral word available; yet at the same time one may note that the contemporary philosopher Alasdair MacIntyre has made of this ordinary word his key to a renewal of the understanding of how moral thinking works.

77. The most thorough effort to ban the notion of "sacrament" is that of Vernard Eller, *In Place of Sacraments: A Study of Baptism and the Lord's Supper* (Grand Rapids: Eerdmans, 1972). I agree with Eller's critique of ritual "religion "and of the medieval "superstitious" or "magical" dimensions of what *sacrament* means in that setting. If we had to let the adversaries write the dictionary, he would be right. I am making the same point Eller does, but I seek to do it in a more affirmative way, keeping or reclaiming the word, (a) by adding three other practices, (b) by defining them sociologically, and (c) by demonstrating how they extrapolate into the "politics" of the rest of the "real world," rather than being confined within a special ritual realm.

78. Other examples would be the love of the enemy (see E on page 46, H on page 76); truth-telling, freeing slaves, serving instead of ruling; cf. below Note 79.

79. In my study *The Politics of Jesus* (Grand Rapids: Eerdmans, 1972), I gave special attention to the ("political") quality of Jesus' ministry, so fully that some have thought the case for enemy love and nonviolence to be my only interest. For that reason I have downplayed it here.

80. Some systems say that the other source of guidance is "reason" or "nature" or "creation"; the various meanings have in common that they bypass Jesus, being known otherwise and calling for other behavior. In correlation with paragraph D on page 45, it might be noted that the "other values" are regularly those appealed to in favor of war: the givenness of national solidarity, the reasonableness of the appeal to superior power, the "realism" of political "effectiveness." Cf. my *The Original Revolution* (Scottdale: Herald, 1977), p. 127.

81. Jonathan Z. Smith, one of the most erudite analysts of religious styles, proposes that we should divide understandings of how God relates to history as either "locative" or "utopian." This is one of many ways in which brilliant analysts can divide their data. I am not sure such splits are needed; perhaps both dimensions can interlock dialectically.

82. Helmut Richard Niebuhr, most widely know for advocating a cultural strategy he called "Christ transforming culture," also wrote part of an important book called *The Church Against the World* (Chicago: Willett and Clark, 1935).